The Secret Gems of Poetry Revealed

Studymates

Studymates

Helping You to Achieve

The Secret Gems of Poetry Revealed

**Edited by
Richard Cochrane**

www.studymates.co.uk

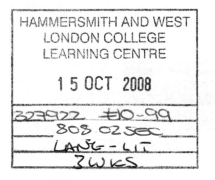
© 2007 by Richard Cochrane
additional material © 2007 Studymates Limited.

ISBN 13 978 1-84285-092-3

First published in 2006 by Studymates Limited.
PO Box 225, Abergele, LL18 9AY, United Kingdom.

Website: http://www.studymates.co.uk

Typeset by Domex e-Data Pvt. Ltd.
Printed and bound in Great Britain by Baskerville Press

Contents

1 What is Poetry?

One-minute overview

No one can offer you a cut-and-dried definition of poetry, but its main feature – in contrast to prose – is its emphasis on form. Poetic form is a kind of structure, in which the words of the poem are set. This analogy isn't perfect, but it's more useful than you might imagine at first.

Important examples of formal elements in poetry are metre, rhyme and the visual structure of the poem. Features like these work together to produce the situation in which 'form enacts content'. This means that the form is just as important as the content in determining the meaning of the poem, and the relationship between the two is a key point for analysis. We end this chapter by looking at some important general skills, which will help you to develop as a literary critic.

In this chapter you will learn:
- what is meant by the term 'poetic form'
- how poetry and prose are related
- how to approach poetry
- the basic skills you need to produce good work
- some avoidable common mistakes.

What Poetry Isn't

Poetry isn't prose. That might sound obvious to you, but ask yourself: why? What's the difference between a poem and a piece of prose? What is it that makes a poem a poem?

Functional Prose

Let's be unsophisticated for a moment. Let's say that a piece of 'straight' prose is a piece of writing that is designed to convey a meaning. Take this, for example:

'No left turn ahead.'

This sentence says that you can't turn left at the next junction. You can say it in all sorts of other ways:

'Do not turn left at the next junction.'
'Turning left is not permitted.'
'Turn right or go straight on.'

The differences are not terribly important; some versions may be clearer than others, but that's the only real reason for choosing one over another. With functional prose, all you want is the information it contains: any version that gives you correct information will aid your understanding.

Literary Prose

As we all know, prose is not only used for giving simple instructions and information. It can also be used to create literature. In that case, the choice of words is of great importance. There is more emphasis on the words themselves, and we're a lot less willing to change them without good reason. Poetry is like this too, but there's one important difference: poems emphasise form.

Don't expect a clear-cut explanation of the difference between poetry and prose. Just as you can have days when it isn't exactly hot or cold, so there are texts that are somewhere between poetry and literary prose. In practice, though, this situation turns out to be extremely unusual.

Turning a Poem into Prose

One way to make this difference clear is to try turning a poem into a piece of prose. Let's take, as an example, 'The Shepherd' by William Blake:

How sweet is the shepherd's sweet lot!

From the morn to the evening he strays;

He shall follow his sheep all the day,

And his tongue shall be filled with praise.

For he hears the lamb's innocent call,

And he hears the ewe's tender reply;

He is watchful while they are in peace,

For they know when their Shepherd is nigh.

This seems pretty simple and direct – it certainly isn't fancy or complicated writing. That simplicity is part of what the poem is about, and it's one of the things that is most likely to strike you about the poem.

If it were a piece of prose, here's what it would look like:

> *How sweet is the shepherd's sweet lot! From the morn to the evening he strays; he shall follow his sheep all the day, and his tongue shall be filled with praise. For he hears the lamb's innocent call, and he hears the ewe's tender reply; he is watchful while they are in peace, for they know when their Shepherd is nigh.*

Suddenly it reads very strangely. Prose rarely uses so many rhymes, and the regular rhythm of the words is odd because prose tends to have a looser, more flexible rhythm that is closer to everyday speech.

This isn't simple and direct any more; it's a complicated, rather peculiar piece of prose. When something is unusual, we tend to sit up and take notice of it – and that's likely to affect our experience of reading the text.

Form and Content

Form and content both depend on the words in the text, and you can change either one by changing the words. Take, for example:

The cat sat on the mat.

You can change the content, like this:

The cat sat near the mat.

This changes the meaning of the text because you've changed the meaning of a word. You can also change the form:

The pussy sat on the rug.

Now the text has lost its three little rhyming words. As a result, its form has been altered, although the sentence still says roughly the same thing. If, instead of being a statement, it were a poem, this might also affect the meaning of the whole text.

Toolkit

The difference between form and content probably still looks pretty confusing. Don't panic: we're going to see a lot more examples of poetic form throughout this book. It might not become familiar in the next five minutes, but it won't take long to get used to how the concept works.

The Nature of Poetic Form

Poetic *form* is a bit like a jelly mould. You can pour any flavour of jelly into the mould – you can even use blancmange – and the effect will be the same.

That is, the *form* will be the same. If you like jelly but hate blancmange, the chances are you'll realise that form isn't everything. In fact, when it comes to food, most of us think content is much more important than form. In poetry, however, form is extremely important.

In a poem, the mould might be very complicated or very simple, but it will give some structure to the text, which prose usually lacks. When you analyse poetry, you'll need to pay at least as much attention to the mould as you do to the jelly.

The Difference Between Poems and Jellies

Our neat little analogy doesn't quite work. The fact is that the concept of a strict, clear-cut distinction between form and content is a bit spurious. So why bother with it? Well, there are at least four good reasons not to throw it away.

1. It's useful. You'll find that you can make very sophisticated analyses using the form/content approach.
2. It's part of the history of poetry. A lot of poems use it in ways that you're likely to miss if you aren't looking for it.
3. It's part of the history of literary criticism. Most critics will assume you're familiar with it, so you need to understand it before you can understand their work.
4. There are plenty of books on the subject of form and content. We shouldn't be too keen to dismiss such a complex issue out of hand.

The Major Elements of Form

In this section, we'll look at the main elements of a poem that can provide a formal structure. They're not the only formal elements, but they'll give you a broad picture of what poetic form is and how it works.

Metre

Remember the poem we looked at near the start of this chapter? One of its most prominent features was its regular rhythm. Prose doesn't normally have a rhythm like this. That doesn't mean prose has no rhythm, just that the rhythms of prose are irregular and flexible.

Rhythm is always important in poetry, but in a lot of poems (particularly the sort written before this century) you'll find something more than just rhythm: you'll find metre. Metre is a regular rhythmic structure.

You'll learn the details of metre – and how to analyse it – in the next two chapters, but let's just take a brief look at this stanza from Shakespeare's 'The Phoenix and the Turtle' (a stanza is what most people call a 'verse' of a poem – a section separated from the rest by blank lines):

Here the anthem doth commence:

Love and constancy is dead,

Phoenix and the turtle fled

In a mutual flame from hence.

Read it aloud with an exaggerated rhythm, so you can hear the metre even if you can't analyse it yet. Now read this stanza aloud:

Property was thus appalled,

That the self was not the same;

Single nature's double name

Neither two nor one was called.

It's from the same poem, and you can probably hear that they have exactly the same rhythm even though the words are completely different. This is our first example of poetic form, and it seems to fit the 'jelly mould' analogy rather well. The structure is the same in each case, even though the words, which have been poured into it, are different.

In the next chapter you'll find out how to take the words away and examine the form itself: the equivalent of removing the jelly so you can get a better look at the mould.

Homophony

You might think 'homophony' sounds like just the kind of obscure, technical terminology designed specifically to confuse you. You'd be wrong. 'Homo' means 'the same' and 'phony' means 'sound', so 'homophony' just means 'the same sound'.

There are many different kinds of homophony in poetry, and we deal with this in more detail in Chapter 4. However, the most common and best-known kind is rhyme. Look at the two stanzas that we saw in the last section. In each case the first and last lines end with words that end in the same sound. This is another formal structure, and you'll soon learn how to separate it from the words of the poem.

Visual structure

The term 'visual structure' describes how the text appears on the page. In most prose – even the literary kind – this isn't a consideration. The text appears as a continuous block of words. In poetry, though, the words are laid out in lines and this often affects the meaning.

Although you don't analyse visual structure directly, you should always be aware of the effect it has on the poem. Imagine if the first of the two stanzas we've just been looking at was written out like this instead:

Here the anthem

Doth commence: love

And constancy is dead, Phoenix

And the turtle fled in a mutual flame

from hence.

Perhaps you can't say why this is different, or exactly what effect it has, but surely you'll agree that the poem has changed. If you're not convinced, imagine you were an editor publishing a book of poems: would it be okay to set the text out on the page like this?

Form Enacting Content

'Form enacting content' is the theme of this whole book, and it's an idea that you'll come to understand gradually, by seeing it happen in different situations.

Look again at the first poem in this chapter – the one we turned into prose. At the time we noticed that both the rhythm and the rhyme system had a simple, plain feel. What might strike you is that the poem is actually about simplicity and innocence. This is exactly what 'form enacting content' is about: it's as if the form were acting out, or imitating, the subject of the poem.

Poetry analysis will not always be so straightforward. If the poem had very complex formal elements, it might leave you puzzling over what looks like a contradiction. The crucial thing to remember is that form and content will always be closely related because they are two aspects of the same poem.

Basic Literary Skills

There are some skills in poetry analysis that are absolutely essential. Without them you're likely to make some very basic mistakes. These skills are:

- close reading
- using evidence to support your claims
- building an argument
- looking for complexity
- avoiding value judgements
- analysing the poem not the poet
- using good, modern editions
- reading around the poem and the poet.

Close Reading

'Close reading' means scrutinising every detail of a text. This is particularly important for poetry. Poems are often extremely short and you will not achieve any understanding if you give them the attention you'd pay to a paragraph in a novel.

Poems are crammed with detail. Examine every word. Squeeze every drop of meaning from the text. In a novel you're unlikely to miss anything crucial if you don't do this; in poetry you will miss crucial and important pieces of information.

Toolkit

When you analyse a poem, your level of enquiry can reach the point where you're asking questions about the nature of language itself. That's how fundamental your reading can be and needs to be. Pursue it to the very limit. If this seems impossible now, don't worry. You'll find plenty of approaches to help you throughout this book.

Using Evidence to Support Your Claims

One mistake that many students make at the start of their careers is to say what they think or feel about a poem without giving evidence. This can be called the 'Pub-Bore tendency'. The Pub Bore talks at great length about his/her opinions without supplying the facts to back them up. You can't argue with the Pub Bore, who prefers unfounded opinions to evidence and rational argument. As a result the audience quietly and politely slips away.

As a literary critic you need to approach your work in a more professional way. If you have something to say about a poem you must provide evidence to shows that you're saying something reasonable, even something enlightening.

Building an Argument

The opposite of the Pub Bore is another caricature that we can call the Anorak. The Anorak rejoices in lists of dry, boring facts, tables of information and complicated charts. The Anorak has forgotten that it's important to make sense of what the poem means, not just what it's made of.

Remember that a poem isn't a puzzle; it's a work of art. Understanding a poem is more than just mapping out metrical structures and rhyme schemes. Your evidence should develop into an analysis of what the poem is about, rather than being scattered here and there without any coherent thread. We'll return to this in more detail in Chapter 11.

Looking for Complexity

In part, the purpose of an essay about a poem is simply to show that the poem is interesting. However, there is more to poetry analysis than simply stating the interest factor of the poem. It's your responsibility as a literary critic to help people to understand why a poem might be fascinating and complex, even if it looks straightforward at first glance. Of course, some poems will make you work harder than others on this.

Avoid the temptation to explain the poem so completely that no one need ever read it again. Incoherence, contradictions, inconsistencies and other obstacles are your friends, not your enemies. They will help you develop your essay into something much more sophisticated.

Avoiding Value Judgements

Having said this, your intention is not to say, 'this is a great poem'. Complexity doesn't always mean greatness. Even if you don't like a poem there will still be plenty of interesting comments you can make about it.

The point to remember is that we're dealing with works of literature here, and your preferences may not be shared by the people reading (and marking) your work:

You	Your reader	Your reader says
Liked the poem	Likes the poem	'Big deal'.
Liked the poem	Doesn't like the poem	'Bad call'
Didn't like the poem	Likes the poem	'Wrong again'
Didn't like the poem	Doesn't like the poem	'So what'?

Analysing the poem not the poet

You're not a psychologist and you're not a biographer. Don't try to use the poem to work out what the poet was thinking or feeling. It's better not to speculate on what the poet intended or wanted to say, because you'll never really know. Make sure you keep to the text of the poem and you won't be misled.

Intentional fallacy

When a critic talks about what the poet means, instead of what the poem means, we say they're using the 'intentional fallacy'; they are assuming that because a poem says something, the poet must have thought it. Knowing a bit about when a poem was written and the style it's written in will often help you, but trying to delve into the author's psychology may lead you to wrong conclusions.

Because of this, critics often use the term 'narrator' instead of 'poet'. The narrator is an imaginary character that speaks the words of the poem; you can say what you like about the narrator, as long as it's supported by the words of the poem, without ever mentioning the poet at all.

Using Good, Modern Editions

'Bargain' editions of poems might look tempting, but check to see what you're getting. A full-price edition will probably have a foreword written by an expert and, more importantly, footnotes.

Why are footnotes important? Well, poems often contain unusual, old-fashioned or just plain obscure words. Unless someone tells you what they mean, you'll be left guessing, as in this stanza from Robert Browning's 'Soliloquy of the Spanish Cloister':

Blasted lay that rose-acacia

We're so proud of! Hy, Zy, Hine!...

'St, there's vespers! Plena gratiâ

Ave, Virgo! Gr-r-r—you swine!

This example shows why it is so important to have a quality edition that contains input from experts in the form of a foreword and footnotes.

Reading Around the Poem and the Poet

Poems can refer to all sorts of things. If you know about the thing the poem's referring to, you'll understand it; if not, you might miss the whole point. That's just life – nobody knows everything – but you can be smart and try to cut down a little on the number of times it happens.

Read introductory books on history, theology, philosophy, painting, music; anything that might be relevant. Don't get bogged down in detail; give yourself a broad, basic education. Knowledge like this is impossible to fake, and if you demonstrate it you're likely to impress your readers.

Tutorial

Starting to Study Poetry

Questions

1. How is reading poetry different from reading prose?
2. List three important elements of poetic form.
3. What's meant by the phrase 'form enacting content'?
4. List the eight basic literary skills that you'll need to take with you throughout your career as a literary critic.

Discussion Points

In most of the discussion points in this book, you'll find it helpful to use a poem to focus the discussion.

- Is form really distinct from content?
- Why does it matter what poems mean?
- Why is it worthwhile to study them?

Practical Assignments

1. Take a line from a poem and try changing one or more words to alter:
   a) just the content
   b) just the form
   c) both
   d) neither.
   Not as easy as it sounds, is it? That's because form and content are so closely related in a piece of poetry.

2. Pick a short poem from an anthology and examine the language as closely as possible. See how much you can spot that you missed on first reading.

3. If you've studied poetry before, dig out your old essays. See if you can identify:
   a) where you were talking about formal elements (probably not too often)
   b) where you were focusing on content (probably most of the time).

2 Regular Metre

One-minute overview

Metre is the rhythmic element of poetry, which is one aspect of poetic form. In the first chapter, we talked about poetic form as a sort of mould into which the words are fitted. A rhythmic structure is one sort of mould that poets use to give form to their writing. Here we'll be looking at regular metres; in the next chapter we'll see how poets use irregularity to create variety and effect subtle changes in meaning.

Just as most music has a strong, regular beat, so does most poetry. Many of the best-known poems – particularly older ones – are actually 'lyrics' that were originally sung to music. Because metre is musical, remember to use your ears as well as your eyes; it will even help if you read the examples in this chapter aloud.

In this chapter you will learn:
- what metres are made up of: syllables, stress and feet
- how to analyse a metrical structure.

What is Metre?

The metre is the overall rhythmic structure of the poem.

Metre is made up of:

- **syllables** – they are composed of a vowel, usually accompanied by one or two consonant sounds
- **a metrical 'foot'** – this is composed of a number of syllables
- **a sequence of 'feet'** – this makes up a metre.

What is a syllable?

Vowels

There are far more vowel sounds than the five letters *a, e, i, o* and *u*. Generally speaking, a vowel is a sound that you can make by breathing through your vocal chords and out of your mouth. Try saying 'ah', 'ooh', 'oh', 'eee', 'air' and 'or'. Make them long sounds and notice how different they are from, say, *p* or *g* (the sounds, not the names of the letters, which end in vowel sounds: 'pee' and 'gee').

Consonants

A consonant is anything that isn't a vowel. Again, remember that we're not just talking about individual letters like *d, m, g, f* and *p*. English contains a lot of what linguists call 'consonantal clusters' like 'str' (as in 'strong'). Each of these, too, is a consonant sound.

Syllables

A syllable is a single beat in the rhythm of speech. Each beat contains a vowel sound and, usually, one or two consonant sounds as well. These are all syllables:

A	Vowel only
Me	Consonant + vowel
On	Vowel + consonant
Cat	Consonant + vowel + consonant
Ship	As above ('sh' is a consonantal cluster)
Gnome	As above (the first and last letters are not pronounced)

Polysyllabic words

We've just seen a list of 'monosyllabic' words – words with only one syllable. Most English words, though, are 'polysyllabic'; they're made of several syllables arranged together.

'London', for example, has two syllables. Say it slowly and deliberately: Lon-don. You should clearly hear two beats, two distinct parts to the word, which make a rhythmic pattern: Lon-don. 'Manchester' has three syllables: Man-ches-ter. 'Nottinghamshire' has four syllables: No-tting-ham-shire. If you'd like to see more examples like this, look in a dictionary: most give a pronunciation guide for each word, which shows its different syllables.

Words with more than four syllables are unusual in English. Although many do exist, they're often obscure or technical terms, like pol-y-syl-ab-ic. The vast majority of English words have one, two or three syllables.

Exceptions

There are some cases of syllables that don't have conventional vowel sounds. Think of 'bubble' – definitely a two-syllable word, bu-bble. Yet the second syllable has no vowel sound in it. Other examples are 'spasm' (spa-sm) and 'riddle' (ri-ddle).

The sounds 'lll', 'rrr' and 'zzz' are a lot like vowels, and in some words – not many – they act as vowels to form a separate syllable. So don't be surprised if you hear two beats but only see one vowel sound: your ears may be right after all.

What is Stress?

Syllables can be either stressed or unstressed. A stressed syllable is emphasised more than an unstressed one. Understanding stress is absolutely essential to being able to analyse metre.

Here are the conventional marks for stress in metrical analysis:

/   stressed syllable

u   unstressed syllable

Spotting the difference between unstressed and stressed syllables gets easier with practice; the rest of this section will help you develop this skill.

Stress in polysyllabic words

Here are some polysyllabic words, with the stressed and unstressed syllables marked. Say the words clearly and slowly to yourself. The secret is to exaggerate the way you say them, so that their rhythmic patterns are all the more obvious:

/   u   u

Pho-to-graph

u   /   u   u

Pho-to-graph-y

/   u   /   u

Pho-to-graph-ic

If you want more examples, pick up the dictionary again; as well as breaking words into syllables, they usually show which syllable should be stressed. There are some general rules.

- A stress never follows another stress.
- More than two unstressed syllables in a row is very rare.
- Words often start with a stressed syllable.

Stress in monosyllabic words

Monosyllabic words can be either stressed or unstressed, depending on their place in the sentence. The general rules for this are similar to those for polysyllabic words.

- Two stresses are rarely found together.
- More than two unstressed words together is unusual.
- More important words are often stressed; words like 'a' and 'the' are usually unstressed.

Let's take a simple sentence containing only monosyllables:

I am a mole and I live in a hole.

Say it (go ahead: no one's listening) and hear the rhythm of the words:

/ u u /   u u / u u /

I am a mole and I live in a hole.

You might like to imagine that the stressed words are written in italics, for added emphasis:

I am a *mole* and I *live* in a *hole*.

Try stressing different words and you'll see that it feels much more natural to say the sentence as it's written above.

> **Toolkit**
>
> Identifying stressed and unstressed syllables will get easier when you have a complete theory of metre, which you will possess by the end of this chapter.
>
> In the meantime, here's a trick to help you check your analyses. Try using 'dum' for stressed and 'da' for unstressed syllables; it emphasises the musical element nicely. 'I am a mole and I live in a hole' would go 'dum da da dum da da dum da da dum'. Just don't let anyone else hear you doing it!

What are Feet?

Armed with what you've already learned, you can go ahead and analyse rhythmic structures, but all you'll get is a bunch of '/'s and 'u's. Let's analyse the first of the stanzas from 'The Turtle and the Phoenix', which we saw in Chapter 1.

Here the anthem doth commence:	/ u / u / u /
Love and constancy is dead,	/ u / u / u /
Phoenix and the turtle fled	/ u / u / u /
In a mutual flame from hence.	/ u / u / u /

The regular rhythm that we noticed when we first read it is obvious from the patterns of stressed and unstressed syllables. Each line goes '/ u / u / u /' (dum da dum da dum da dum), but that doesn't really tell us much about the poem.

What we need to do is break this down into 'feet'. A foot is a unit of two or three syllables – usually a mixture of stressed and unstressed – which is repeated to make a regular rhythm. There are four basic kinds.

Iamb

Pronounced 'eye-am', this foot has one unstressed syllable followed by one stressed syllable, as in this line from Andrew Marvell's 'The Fair Singer':

u /	u /	u /	u /	u /
I could	have fled	from one	but sing-	-ly fair

Try saying the line repeatedly to get a feel for the rhythm.

Trochee

Pronounced 'troe-key', (the adjective is 'trochaic') this foot has one stressed syllable followed by one unstressed syllable – like a reversed iamb. Here's an example from Henry David Thoreau's 'Low-Anchored Cloud':

/ u	/ u	/ u	/ u
Foun-tain	head and	source of	ri-vers

Anapaest

The anapaest (pronounced 'an-a-pest') has three syllables: two unstressed followed by one stressed. It's much less common than the trochee or iamb. Here's an example from Lord Byron's 'The Destruction of Sennacherib':

u u / u u / u u / u u /

The Assyrian came down like the wolf on the fold

Repeat the line over and over and you'll soon hear the three-beat rhythm of this foot.

Dactyl

Pronounced 'dak-till', this is another three-syllable foot. It's exactly the opposite of an anapest, as shown in this line from Thomas Hardy's 'The Voice':

/ u	/ u	/ u	/
Hera the	An-them	Doth co-	-mence

u	/ u	/ u	/ u	/ u
And	Love and	Con-stan-	-cy is	dead

The three-syllable feet are much less common than the iamb and trochee.

Number of feet per line

The number of feet in a line is indicated by the following words:

Monometer	one foot	(very rare)
Bimeter	two feet	(very rare)
Trimeter	three feet	(quite unusual)
Quatrameter	four feet	(very common)
Pentameter	five feet	(very common)
Hexameter	six feet	(quite common)
Heptameter	seven feet	(quite unusual)
Octameter	eight feet	(unusual)
Nonameter	nine feet	(quite rare)
Decameter	ten feet	(very rare)

So 'iambic pentameter' (the most common metre of all) has five iambs in each line. You needn't memorise all these technical terms straight away: understanding the general concept – that poetic metre is a rhythm made up of repeated units – is much more important.

Variations on the Classical Feet

Trailing syllables

Trailing syllables come at the end of a line, and aren't part of a foot; they're sometimes referred to as 'extra-metrical' or 'hypermetrical'. In 'The Phoenix and the Turtle', Shakespeare has added a trailing stress to the end of each line:

/ u	/ u	/ u	/
Here the	an-them	doth com-	-mence

This may have been designed to give each line a firm ending – what used to be called a 'masculine' ending.

He does the opposite in Hamlet's famous speech, the first line of which goes like this:

/ u u	/ u u	/ u u	/ u u
Wo-man much	missed, how you	call to me,	call to me

Here, the iambic feet (u /) are finished off by an unstressed syllable; this was once called a 'feminine' ending. In Shakespeare's time, this was thought to be weaker and more uncertain than the masculine ending (in which the line finishes with a stress).

> **Note**
> You might not be completely convinced by this version of the stresses in Hamlet's line. We will discuss a more sophisticated version in the next chapter.

Although the term comes from French grammar, the idea that women are weak and uncertain, and men are rational and strong, is definitely implied when someone uses the term 'feminine' or 'masculine' ending.

Leading syllables

A leading syllable comes at the start of a line, and like the trailing version it's not part of a metrical foot. They're almost always unstressed; that's just the way that metre tends to work. A classic example of a leading syllable is an 'and' placed at the start of a line. Imagine if Shakespeare had written this:

u / u / u / u / u /

No longer mourn for me when I am dead

u / u / u / u / u /

And then you shall hear the surly sullen bell

U / u / u / u / u /

Give warning to the world that I am fled

u / u / u / u / u /

From this vile world, with vilest worms to dwell:

Because of the regularity of the surrounding poem, we can easily think of the 'and' on line two as an addition that isn't part of the regular metrical structure of the line as a whole.

Because leading syllables tend to be unstressed, this is not such a good analysis of Shakespeare's metre:

/ u / u / u / u /

And then you shall hear the surly sullen bell

The first syllable just sounds too important to be an added extra. If the surrounding lines were all in trochees without leading syllables, then it might make more sense, but as a regular feature it's not too convincing.

> **Note**
>
> Actually, leading and trailing syllables are often examples of irregularities, but sometimes they're used regularly throughout a poem, as in 'The Phoenix and the Turtle'.

Elision

'Elision' means compressing two syllables into one by missing out (eliding) one of the vowel sounds. Everyday examples include 'can't', 'it's' and 'I'm'. Common poetic ones include 't'was' (it was) and the contraction of 'the' to 'th' as in 'th' inn', which makes 'the inn' (two syllables) into a one-syllable unit.

More subtle effects of elision come when a regular metre encourages the reader to elide a sound even when there's no indication (like an apostrophe). Take the first line of 'The Destruction of Sennacherib':

u u / u u / u u / u u /

The Assyrian came down like the wolf on the fold

Here, the word 'Assyrian' is scanned as u / u ('A-ssyr-ian'), but say the word on its own and you're much more likely to say 'A-ssyr-i-an' – four syllables, u / u u. Read the whole line with this pronunciation, though, and it sounds quite wrong; the overall rhythm encourages the reader to squeeze the two vowel sounds together to form a single syllable.

More Complex Metres

The metre of a poem is its overall, general rhythmic structure. 'The Phoenix and the Turtle' has a very simple metre: trochaic trimeter with a trailing stress (| / u | / u | / u | / | if you want to be technical, or 'dum da dum da dum da dum' if you're lecturing the local nursery school). Always use the technical version in essays.

Other poems often have more complex metres. This is a slightly less simple one – an excerpt from Thomas Gray's 'Ode on the Death of a Favourite Cat':

u / u / u / u /

'Twas on a lofty vase's side,

u / u / u / u /

Where China's gayest art had dyed

u / u / u /

The azure flowers that blow;

u / u / u / u /

Demurest of the tabby kind,

u / u / u / u /

The pensive Selima, reclined,

u / u / u /

Gazed on the lake below.

The structure here is two lines of iambic quatrameter (four iambs, u /) followed by one line of iambic trimeter (just three feet). This pattern continues throughout the poem.

Notice that the structure actually tells you how to pronounce the cat's name. You might have been tempted to say 'Se-li-ma' , like 'Selina', but Gray implies that the proper stresses fall on the first and last syllables, 'Se-li-ma'. This makes her seem much more exotic, because it's an unusual pattern for an English word.

> **Note**
> You might not feel that this analysis of the last line is correct. Read it aloud. It's passable, but the first two words feel awkward – '*Gazed on the lake be-low*'. We'll see how to make a better version in the next chapter.

Regular Metre in Context

A Short History of Metre

Here are some key periods in the development of metre:

- **Around 1400–1700:** The Renaissance, and the introduction to England of 'syllabic metre'. Poems began to follow strict metrical patterns.
- **Around 1700–1850:** The Augustans and Romantics developed the use of looser overall structures – for example, iambic pentameter with the odd line of trimeter – but within each line the metre was still adhered to relatively closely.
- **Around 1850–1920:** Gradually, poets began experimenting with more and more irregular metrical systems until, with the rise of Modernism, some abandoned regular metres entirely. After 1920 poets developed in various ways, but it's fair to say that metrical poetry in the 20th century always feels either popular and folksy (e.g. the British comedic poet Pam Ayres) or traditional (like A.E. Housman).

What is Regular Metre?

Syllabic metre was relatively new in the Renaissance, so following its rules was a sign of sophistication. The arts in the Renaissance generally had a tendency towards formality; the word 'renaissance' means rebirth, referring to the rediscovery of ancient Greek art, science and philosophy. With that came creative work, which valued formal relationships more than ever before in Europe.

By the time of the Romantics (1790–1830), regular metre had become rather old fashioned. Sophistication came to be linked with a different kind of complexity: skilful variations on metrical structures. The Romantics (e.g. Blake and Wordsworth) tended to revere nature; think of the natural world's tendency to produce many variations on a single design, and you will see how poets used the same idea of many variations on a single design in their poetry.

'The Phoenix and the Turtle' is a serious poem, given a stately rhythm by those trailing stresses we discussed earlier. The regularity of the metre is a part of its rather intellectual, formal style. In Blake's 'The Shepherd', though, the rural innocence it describes is enacted by its formal simplicity. Both have regular metres, but the meanings of these metres are quite different.

> **Toolkit**
>
> You can see that knowing when a poem was written is important here. Sometimes – as in some 'unseen' exams – you won't have that knowledge. In that case don't risk any assumptions. The more poetry you read the better you'll get at recognising work from different periods, often by the words used and the subject matter. If you're unsure, don't leap to any conclusions about regular metres: you may be well off the mark.

Summary

Metrical analysis is full of technical terms. Don't be put off by them: no one is going to be overly impressed just because you can say 'anapaestic hexameter' anyway. What will impress is your ability to use this information to understand the poem – something we'll come to shortly.

Here's a quick run-down of the terms defined in this section:

- **Foot:** a collection of two or three syllables, usually one stressed and the others unstressed. The common ones are trochee, iamb, dactyl and anapest.
- **Trailing syllable:** a syllable at the end of a line, which isn't part of a metrical foot.
- **Leading syllable:** a syllable at the start of a line, which isn't part of a metrical foot.
- **Masculine ending:** a line that ends with a stressed syllable – traditionally a 'strong' ending that suggests completion.
- **Feminine ending:** a line that ends with an unstressed syllable – traditionally a weaker, more uncertain resolution.
- **Elision:** missing out a vowel sound to create the desired rhythmic effect.

Tutorial

Studying Regular Metre
Questions

1. What are the four most common metrical feet?
2. List the three broad historical periods in the history of English metrical poetry.
3. What are leading and trailing syllables? (Try to find examples.)
4. What are masculine and feminine endings?
5. What is elision?

Discussion Points

- Is there always one correct metrical analysis for any line of poetry? If not, how can you decide which one to use?

Practical Assignment

Think of some nursery rhymes and work out their metrical structures (they tend to be very regular). You can do the same with many pop songs.

Study Tips
- Use a dictionary to check your analyses of polysyllabic words.
- Practice is the key to getting the hang of metrical analysis. Work on it every day if you find it difficult, and it will soon become easy.

3 | Metrical Irregularities

One-minute overview

If all poems went 'dum da dum da dum' and so on, then the rhythmic side of poetry would be very boring. Fortunately, almost all poems use irregularities to vary the rhythm and make the poem more interesting. The irregularities also give the critic (that's you) a chance to find extra, subtle alterations in meaning in the poem, which are valuable when you come to writing your essays.

Always remember that it is 'meaning' in the poem that is essential: if you can't say how one of these formal features affects the meaning of the poem you're looking at, it's not worth mentioning it. Few examiners hand out marks for spotting spondees (see below) and enjambment, if you can't say anything except 'Look! There's one!' Remember, too, that memorising all of these technical words isn't the point; the point is seeing an irregularity and saying what it means.

In this chapter you will learn:

■ how to spot and understand irregularities in metrical poems
■ how to handle free verse
■ to further develop your understanding of metre and meaning.

Irregularities in Metrical Verse

Underlying Metre

The concept of 'underlying metre' is a very useful one. When poets introduce irregularities in their metres they are not normally changing the structure itself, just making a variation on it.

Some poems have a very subtle underlying metre with many variations to give it an elastic, unpredictable movement. The more irregularities there are, the more likely it is that the poem is from a later historical period, although this is a guideline rather than a rule.

Substitution of Feet

Often, poets substitute one foot for another to give some variety. This can be quite surprising, drawing special attention to the word or words that cause the irregularity.

You might not, for instance, agree with my original 'scanning' of the last line of Gray's stanza:

u /	u /	u /
Gazed on	the lake	be-low

I wrote it that way to make the example clearer, but this is much better:

/ u	/ u	/ u
Gazed on	the lake	be-low

The first trochee has been replaced by an iamb. Notice the very different rhythmic feel this gives the line: 'dum da-da dum da dum' instead of 'da dum da dum da dum'. You'll see one of the effects this has in a moment.

> **Note**
> When the stress pattern of a foot is reversed – turning | u / | into | / u |, for example – this is sometimes called 'inversion' or 'reversion'.

Addition or Removal of Feet

Sometimes, variation of the metrical length of lines is part of the regular structure, as in the short lines in Gray's 'Ode on the Death of a Favourite Cat'. Other times, you'll find short lines interspersed just for variety, or for dramatic effect, and it can be quite startling when a line unexpectedly comes to an abrupt stop.

Additional feet can feature in exactly the same way. Often a longer line is used to tie up an idea and give a sense of finality, as if the extra foot or two put a cap on the matter, as satirised here in Alexander Pope's 'Essay on Criticism':

Then, at the last and only couplet fraught

With some unmeaning thing they call a thought,

A needless Alexandrine ends the song

That, like a wounded snake, drags its slow length along.

'Alexandrine' is an old-fashioned name for a line of iambic hexameter – i.e. one iamb more than the underlying metre. At other times the effect will be quite different: a lot depends on the content and the surrounding metrical structure.

The use of 'foreshortened' and 'elongated' lines as irregularities (not regular features) began in the Augustan and Romantic periods. They're not a common feature of earlier writing.

Caesura

A 'caesura' is a pause or break in the metre, usually caused by two stresses coming side by side. 'The Phoenix and the Turtle' could be said to contain a caesura between each line, since each line starts and finishes with a stress. When you read the poem aloud you might find each line feels quite separate from the others because of the pauses that the stresses force you to put between them; this is the main reason why its pace seems so slow and stately.

Usually, though, a caesura is an irregular feature making the poem grind to a halt before it gets itself re-started again. Look at the last two lines of Gray's stanza:

u /	u /	u /	u /
The pen-	-sive Sel-	-i-ma	re-clined

u /	u /	u /
Gazed on	the lake	be-low

We know that the poem is about the death of the cat. The hesitation between the two stresses, followed by the unexpected rush of the two unstressed syllables, enact the precarious position of the cat – a bit like the moving camera in an action sequence of a film.

Caesurae (that's the plural) are often made more effective by the use of long syllables like 'lined' and 'gazed'. Most syllables are short, punchy sounds; longer ones tend to draw out and slow the rhythm anyway, which makes the caesura more effective.

One last example. Many people would read Hamlet's famous line like this:

u /	u /	u /	/ u u	/ u
To be	or not	to be	that is the	ques-tion

The underlying metre of *Hamlet* is iambic pentameter, and so the version we gave at first wasn't unreasonable, but this one is more accurate. By substituting a dactyl for the fourth iamb and a trochee for the fifth, Shakespeare manages to get a caesura at the comma as well as a feminine ending. You might say this enacts the stumbling uncertainty of the speech as a whole.

Spondees and Pyrrhics

Spondees and pyrrhics are special kinds of metrical foot:

Spondee   / /

Pyrrhic   u u

They're never used in regular metres, but sometimes they appear as variations and when they do they often cause dramatic rhythmic changes. A rare example of a line wholly in spondees is Samuel Taylor Coleridge's '*Slow spondee stalks, strong foot*' – though even here it would be more usual to read 'spondee' as / u.

The spondee normally serves to slow the poem down, as in this line from Gerard Manley Hopkins' 'God's Grandeur':

/ u	/ u	u /	/ /	u /
Is bare	now, nor	can foot	feel, be-	-ing shod

The underlying metre is iambic pentameter (this is easier to work out when you can see the whole poem), but the second foot is a trochee and the fourth a spondee. This creates a situation in which the stresses crowd together.

Here, each word in the spondee takes on added weight by virtue of all those stressed syllables. A pyrrhic, on the other hand, usually speeds the line along as if cramming extra words into the metrical scheme, which tends to emphasise the next stressed syllable.

A spondee might or might not create a caesura; the line from Hopkins is so crammed with stresses that there doesn't seem to be a definite pause so much as a general slowing down.

A pyrrhic can produce a caesura, too. Compare Hamlet's line with Henry IV's famous war-cry:

/ /	u u	u /	u /	u /
Cry ha-	-voc and	Let slip	The dogs	Of war

Here the first iamb is replaced by a spondee, and the next becomes a pyrrhic, partly for variety and partly to give even more emphasis to the spondee. The result is that most actors like to shout the first two words and then pause in the middle of the pyrrhic before continuing. The three unstressed syllables in a row are enough to create a caesura; its exact placing is determined by the way the words fit into the formal scheme.

Foregrounding

Effects like caesura and substituted feet often make the word(s) involved more noticeable than the surrounding text. Literary critics call this 'foregrounding'. The results can be very subtle: you'll need to pay attention to the content as well as the form in order to make much sense of them.

Free Verse

The common perception is that free verse is verse without any rhythm; it isn't. All language has rhythmic elements; free verse just doesn't have a regular, repetitive one.

Many poems that look like free verse actually have metrical structures. Whenever you see a free verse poem, quickly jot down an analysis: you might be surprised. The most unlikely poems turn out to have perfectly regular – if rather weird – underlying metres.

Metrical Patterns

If there is no overall metrical form to the poem, perhaps there are little areas of metre – a few lines of iambic pentameter, for instance, tucked away among the rhythmic chaos. T.S. Eliot's 'The Waste Land' is a famous free-verse poem, most of which is actually written in regular metres.

This can serve to set certain lines apart from the rest of the writing; it can also remind the reader of more traditional writing. In 'The Waste Land', all kinds of different poetic styles are jumbled together to reflect the confused state of poetry at the time Eliot was writing.

Alternatively, you might find a loose metrical arrangement, as in 'Low-Anchored Cloud' by Henry David Thoreau:

| / u u | /...

Low-anchored cloud,

| / u u | /...

Newfoundland air,

|/ u | / u | / u | / u |

Fountainhead and source of rivers,

|/ u | / / | u u |

Dew-cloth, dream drapery,

| u / | u / | u / |

And napkin spread by fays;

| / u | / u | / u | /...

Drifting meadow of the air

...u | / u | / u | / u | / u | u...

Where bloom the daisied banks and violets,

u / | u / | u / | u /

And in whose fenny labyrinth

u / | u / | u / | u /

The bittern booms and heron wades;

| / u u | / u | / u | / u |

Spirit of lakes and seas and rivers,

.../ | / u | / u | u / |

Bear only perfumes and scent

| u / | u / | u / | u / |

Of healing herbs to just men's fields!

Metre helps give shape to this poem. It would be confusing and monotonous if it were all in one metre. Instead Thoreau does this:

> 2 anapaestic lines
> 2 trochaic lines
> 1 iambic line
> 1 trochaic line
> an ambiguous line, which is closer to trochees than iambs
> 2 iambic lines
> 2 trochaic lines, the first starting with an anapaest
> 1 iambic line

This, at the very least, gives the poem some variety as a way to overcome its lack of action. The anapaests at the start even get a reprise, like an introduction from a song coming back before the end. Notice the regularity of metre within each line: a trochaic line typically only contains trochees, and so on (with the exception of line 4). Further, each line is in either trimeter or quatrameter. The regularity within each line contrasts with the irregularity of the poem as a whole.

No Metrical Form

Even when there are no regular metrical features you shouldn't forget about rhythm entirely. You can still talk about the use of spondees and pyrrhics to slow down or speed up the pace of a line, and you can still find caesurae and note which words they serve to emphasise. You can also look for short, staccato lines that have a quick, simple delivery, and contrast them with long, rhythmically varied lines whose content is likely to be quite different.

Tutorial

Studying Metrical Irregularities

Questions

1. What are spondees and pyrrhics?
2. What are leading and trailing syllables? (try to find examples.)
3. What is foregrounding?
4. Look at the second stanza of Matthew Arnold's 'Dover Beach' (don't worry about what these lines mean: they're taken out of context and look pretty obscure on their own).

   | / u u | / u | / ...

   Sophocles long ago

   | / u | / u u | / u | / u | / ...

   Heard it on the Aegean, and it brought

   | / u u | / u | / u | / u | / ...

   Into his mind the turbid ebb and flow

   | u / | u / | u / | / ...

   Of human misery; we

   | u / | u / | u / | u / |

   Find also in the sound a thought,

   | / u u | / u | / u | / u | / ...

   Hearing it by this distant northern sea.

   Try to make sense of this irregular metre – or is it actually free verse?
5. Here's Alexander Pope having a laugh at the expense of poets who over-use these tricks, but illustrating them rather well.

> *When Ajax strives some rock's vast weight to throw,*
>
> *The line too labours, and the words move slow;*
>
> *Not so when swift Camilla scours the plain,*
>
> *Flies o'er the unbending corn, and skims along the main.*

Make your own metrical analysis of these lines, with comments.

Discussion Points

- Should all poetry be metrical, or is free verse a more 'natural' form of expression?
- If you take away metre and rhyme, doesn't a poem just turn into a piece of prose written out in a funny or absurd way?

Practical Assignments

1. Compare and contrast the metrical structures of short poems by Shakespeare, Milton, Wordsworth, Gerard Manley Hopkins, Ezra Pound and William Carlos Williams.
2. Find some regular poems (like the nursery rhymes and songs you used in the last chapter) and change them to introduce irregularities like caesurae, spondees, pyrrhics, leading and trailing syllables, elision and substituted feet.

Study Tip

Practice, practice, practice. Always keep an ear out for a verse form you could analyse – even advertising jingles can give you something to think about.

---

4   **Homophony**

One-minute overview

Homophony means 'the same sound'. The best-known form of homophony is rhyme, but there are other kinds too. Homophony is another element of poetic form.

Homophony can be used regularly, as part of a poem's overall structure, or it can be used as a local variation. As with metre, the presence or absence of homophony can have an impact on what the words mean and how you interpret them.

In this chapter you will learn:
- what homophony means
- the different types of homophony
- the relationship between homophony and structure
- how to do a homophonic analysis.

What is Homophony?

Homophony means 'the same sound'. Words have a homophonic relationship if they share sounds in common. For example, 'sun' and 'swat' are homophonic in the sense that they share the same initial sound, 's'. So are 'walk' and 'torn', because of the vowel sounds being the same.

Homophony, like metre, is about sound, not letters. So 'sun' and 'sheet' don't have a homophonic relationship even though they begin with the same letter because they share no sounds in common.

Types of Homophony

Basically, two words can share:

- consonant sounds
- vowel sounds
- both consonant sounds and vowel sounds.

In this section you'll find examples and explanations of all common forms of homophony.

> **Note**
> If you're not sure about vowels, consonants, syllables and so on, see the section 'What is Metre?' in Chapter 2.

Rhyme

Rhyme is the best known of the homophonic structures used in poetry, but it's actually rather complicated. Here's the definition: **Two words rhyme if the portions from the vowel sound of the last stressed syllable to the end of the words sound identical.**

That's a bit complex, so let's start with something simple, like two monosyllabic words: 'lapse' and 'maps'. These words rhyme because from the vowel sound to the end of the word they have identical sounds: 'aps'.

Now take a polysyllabic word: 'perhaps'. The stress falls on the second syllable: 'per-<u>haps</u>'. It rhymes with 'lapse' and 'maps' because everything before the vowel sound of the stressed syllable is ignored.

The identification of the stressed syllable is important. 'Handicaps' doesn't rhyme with any of these words, because the stress falls on the first syllable: '<u>han</u>-di-caps'.

Perfect and imperfect rhymes

This is the rule for perfect rhyming. Poets sometimes use imperfect rhymes (like maps / handicaps) for effect – and you'll see what this might mean later. You'll also sometimes find imperfect rhymes used simply because the poet was unable to find a suitable word to make a perfect rhyme.

Remember, poets aren't slavishly following a recipe when they write poems; sometimes the perfect rhyme just isn't as important as exactly the right word. Complete adherence to perfect rhyming is sometimes considered a sign of unsophisticated, unimaginative writing, like greeting-card doggerel (the writing found in birthday cards or festival cards). Rhymes can certainly become clichés, as Pope remarks in his 'Essay on Criticism':

If crystal streams 'with pleasing murmurs creep,'

The reader's threatened (not in vain) with 'sleep'.

As a rule, the later the poem, the more clichéd lines like this will feel.

Assonance and Consonance

The lead character in Willie Russell *Educating Rita* calls assonance 'getting the rhyme wrong', which as a statement does have a certain level of truth in it. A more formal definition would be *the sharing of vowel sounds but not consonant sounds*. 'Torn' and 'moor' share assonance because their vowel sounds are the same, but they don't rhyme because of the 'n' sound at the end of 'torn'.

In the same manner, consonance is *the sharing of consonant sounds but not vowel sounds*. 'Torn' and 'mine' share consonance because of the 'n' sound they both end in, but they don't rhyme because they don't have the same vowel sounds.

Spotting assonance and consonance through collocation

Assonance and consonance are everywhere, of course, because there are only so many sounds in the English language. What you're looking for is an effect, something that seems significant. Often this will be because the words come next to each other.

Break, break, break

On thy cold grey stones, O Sea!

Here the 'o' sounds in 'cold', 'stones' and, of course, 'O', are identical. It's fair to say that three identical vowel sounds in such a short line is no coincidence. This is called 'collocation' (co-location – being in the same place) and it's one way in which poets use assonance and consonance.

Para-rhyme

The fact that assonance and consonance are like 'getting the rhyme wrong' has led some poets – particularly in the 20th century – to use them instead of rhyme. In general this is thought to make the poem feel discordant and uncomfortable, as in these lines from Wilfred Owen's 'Strange Meeting':

It seemed that out of battle I escaped

Down some profound dull tunnel, long since scooped

Through granites which titanic wars had groined.

Yet also there encumbered sleepers groaned,

Instead of the expected perfect rhymes, each pair of lines ends with a consonance. In many cases, Owen uses consonance at both ends of the words – gr-oi-n'd, gr-oa-n'd – to make it obvious that this is not just a coincidence. He also uses mainly monosyllabic words, which is a common way to draw attention to assonance and consonance.

Alliteration

Alliteration simply means starting with the same sound, like this:

I sing of brooks, of blossoms, birds and bowers

It's usually used to draw words together. Slogans, catchphrases, newspaper headlines and the names of products all regularly use alliteration to make several words sound unified: think of 'safe and sound', 'rock and roll' or 'Kit Kat'. Radio DJs and tabloid journalists also use alliteration; one radio DJ always started his programmes with 'It's Graham with the gramophones – the Welshman's on the wireless'.

Onomatopoeia

This is a tricky one to spell; what it essentially means is words imitating non-linguistic sounds. Onomatopoeia is a kind of poetic sound effect: the word actually sounds like what it means. There are plenty of words in the English language that we commonly think of as onomatopoeic: splash, ding, screech, scream, flutter, slide, drip and bang are just a few examples.

Poetic onomatopoeia often uses words that we don't usually think of this way to create a sound effect. Here's Wilfred Owen again:

Only the stuttering rifles' rapid rattle

Can patter out their hasty orisons.

This is clever stuff, because Owen uses three words that we might usually think of as onomatopoeic ('stuttering', 'rattle', 'patter'), but through alliteration he also draws in the words 'rifles' rapid'. The effect is onomatopoeic even though 'rifle' and 'rapid' aren't normally thought of as sound-effect words.

A word of warning

Students sometimes think onomatopoeia is a natural effect: the words just sound like what they mean, and that's that. In fact, it can only work though convention. That's why Owen uses conventional onomatopoeic words *and* alliteration to make sure we notice the effect. If you aren't sure whether an onomatopoeic effect is present, it's best to assume it's not, or to mention it as a possibility (this is fine: you don't have to be dogmatic about everything).

Homophony and Structure

Homophony is a part of a poem's form, but so far we haven't heard much about how it affects the poem's meaning. To get to this, we'll need to look at how homophony can relate to the structure of a poem.

Rhyme Schemes

The most familiar sort of homophonic structure is the rhyme scheme. This is a regular pattern of rhyming, which the poet uses very much like a regular metre. Let's return to Shakespeare:

Here the anthem doth commence:

Love and constancy is dead,

Phoenix and the turtle fled

In a mutual flame from hence.

The first line rhymes with the fourth, and the second line rhymes with the third. This pattern is continued throughout the first section of the poem.

In more recent (late 19th century onwards) poetry, like Wilfred Owen's 'Strange Meeting' assonance and/or consonance can replace rhymes, but otherwise the rhyme scheme is the only regular, structural homophony you'll find in a poem.

Blank Verse

Not all poems have rhyme schemes. Many 20th-century poets have rejected rhyme as a structural tool, but unlike metre, non-rhyming poetry has always been around. The most common sort is 'blank verse'. People sometimes think this means the same as 'free verse', but it doesn't: it specifically refers to non-rhyming iambic pentameter. Virtually all of Shakespeare's plays are written in blank verse, and the form has remained very popular. So even if a poem is fairly old, don't imagine that it must have a rhyme scheme: some (especially longer ones) do not.

Rhyme-Scheme Irregularities

Unlike metres, rhyme schemes tend to be extremely regular. Poets rarely use assonance or consonance instead of a full rhyme, and the result is often felt to be an imperfection rather than a deliberate effect.

Distorted pronunciation

Rhyme schemes are so regular that sometimes a poet will choose to distort the pronunciation of a word to make it fit. Look at these lines by Robert Herrick, from an erotic poem about dishevelled clothing:

A sweet disorder in the dress

Kindles in clothes a wantonness.

A lawn about the shoulders thrown

Into a fine distractiön;

According to the rhyme scheme, these are supposed to rhyme. If the umlaut (two dots) over the 'o' wasn't there, we would say that this was a rather startling homophonic and metrical irregularity.

Instead, though, it looks as if Herrick is trying to encourage us to pronounce it 'dis-*trac*-she-*ohn*'. This has two effects. In the first place, it's closer to the French pronunciation and this would have carried connotations of erotic sophistication (as it still does, to some extent, today). The second effect is one of form enacting content: the disorganised clothing that Herrick finds so exciting is enacted by this disorganised bit of poetry. Distorted pronunciation is also very often a humorous effect, something like the performance of a deliberately awkward clown, as it may be here (you'd have to look at the rest of the poem to decide).

Non-structural Homophony

Homophony other than rhyme is rarely used in a repetitive, predictable way; it comes up at odd moments and leaves you wondering whether or not it's relevant.

The question you should always ask yourself is not:

Did the author intend it? but,

Does it affect my understanding of the poem?

You'll never know what the author intended in most cases anyway, but you can look for clues as to whether you're seeing a significant effect or just a random feature. The best clue is collocation: if you see several homophonic effects close together, it's likely that your attention will be drawn to them, and that in itself makes them significant.

Analysing a Rhyme Scheme

It's very easy to analyse rhyme schemes; you're looking for a group of lines with a structure that then repeats itself. Going step by step, you:

- identify the rhymes
- look for repeated units
- check for structural variations.

Identify the Rhymes

Let's take 'The Phoenix and the Turtle' again:

Here the anthem doth commence:

Love and constancy is dead,

Phoenix and the turtle fled

In a mutual flame from hence.

Here you know that 'commence' rhymes with 'hence' and that 'dead' rhymes with 'fled'. So, mark the first group of rhyming words 'A' and the second group 'B'. 'A' rhymes are those that sound like 'ence' and 'B' rhymes are those that sound like 'ed'.

Here the anthem doth commence:	A
Love and constancy is dead,	B
Phoenix and the turtle fled	B
In a mutual flame from hence.	A

Look for Repeated Units

If the poem were only four lines long, we'd be finished: we'd say it rhymed ABBA. However, there are 18 separate stanzas in 'The Phoenix and the Turtle'. Here's the one after the one we just analysed:

So they loved as love in twain

Had the essence but in one;

Two distincts, division none:

Number there in love was slain.

You have to know that 'one' rhymed with 'none' in Shakespeare's time – or, at least, that was the poetic convention, and it's a convention which poets and songwriters still use today even though many people no longer pronounce these two words the same way.

Once you know that, you can see that this stanza rhymes 'CDDC' according to our analysis:

A -*ence*

B -*ed*

C -*ain*

D -*one*

But CDDC and ABBA are exactly the same things; they just mean that the fourth line rhymes with the first and the second with the third. So, if the whole poem were like this we would simply say it was written in four-line stanzas rhyming ABBA.

Check for Structural Variations

If there is the odd word that doesn't rhyme perfectly, you'd say this was an irregularity, but you wouldn't say it was part of the form of the poem. However, it's important to check that the poem doesn't change. 'The Phoenix and the Turtle' stays with ABBA right up until the end, which goes like this:

Beauty, truth and rarity,

Grace in all simplicity,

Here enclosed in cinders lie.

Death is now the phoenix' nest

And the turtle's loyal breast

To eternity doth rest,

Leaving no posterity:

'Twas not their infirmity,

It was married chastity.

The rhyme scheme is simply AAA. The first stanza seems to contain an imperfect rhyme ('*rar*-i-ty' doesn't rhyme with 'sim-*pli*-ci-ty' because of stress) and 'lie', which rhymes with neither. In Shakespeare's time, though, it was a convention that the ending '-ity' could be pronounced '-i-*tie*' (hence '*rar*-i-tie', 'sim-*pli*-ci-*tie*').

These were clearly irregularities, not structural features, because of the regularity of the rest of the poem.

No Overall Structure

When there's no overall structure, it is sometimes possible in poems to find repeated cells or units which might or might not give you a vague formal element. This, in turn might or might not be useful. It's always worth checking and spending five minutes to see what you can find.

Here's the rhyme scheme for Matthew Arnold's 'Dover Beach':

ABA C DBD C EF C GFG	(stanza 1)
ABA CBC	(stanza 2)
ABCDBEDC	(stanza 3)
ABBA CDDC C	(stanza 4)

As you can see, it has no regular pattern in terms of repeated stanzas. It does, however, have a tendency towards ABA-type patterns; the first stanza contains three of these and the second has two. These are then expanded into ABBA patterns for the last stanza. The third stanza seems completely random, though rhyme is still used, as if to loosely bind the lines together.

If you did your assignment at the end of Chaper 1, you'll know that 'Dover Beach' uses metre in a very fragmented, distorted way, but it doesn't totally ignore it. In the same way, Arnold uses fragments of a rhyme scheme in a rather disorientating manner (and one that was ground breaking for 1867).

If you know the poem's content, you might also feel that the more regular final stanza enacts the element of hope that it contains, in contrast to the panic and despair that goes before it. Could it be that Arnold's ABAs, those fragments of traditional poetic practice, are re-cast as ABBAs at the end, enacting a fresh hope in the face of chaos? That's not something you'd say lightly, but in the context of an analysis it might be justified.

Summary

We've already seen a lot of examples of homophony being meaningful, but a recap of the most important ones will be useful.

Foregrounding

As we've already seen, 'foregrounding' is just a technical term for 'drawing attention to'. Homophony can foreground words in the middles of lines, making them stand out. The absence of a rhyme where you expect one – whether it's replaced by assonance or consonance or no homophony at all – can also foreground the guilty word, just as an off-key note stands out even in a whole orchestra.

Association

Associated words are words that sound like each other and might *be* like each other. This is how alliteration works to bind a group of words together. Here's Gerard Manley Hopkins again:

As kingfishers catch fire, dragonflies draw flame;

The line is virtually broken in half at the comma because of the alliteration on each side, which unifies the words (and also the caesura, which you might have spotted). This is useful to Hopkins, of course, because neither kingfishers nor dragonflies are particularly flammable. The alliteration makes the image more acceptable because it makes it seem slightly more natural.

In just the same way the old advertising slogan

'*My goodness, my Guinness!*' attempted to make a connection between the alcoholic beverage and physical health. It was more sophisticated than the alliterative '*Guinness is good for you*' (an earlier slogan) because the homophony was stronger ('My g–ness, my g–ness') and the effect more subtle. Note that the phrase 'My goodness, my Guinness' doesn't actually claim that Guinness has any health-enhancing properties – the suggestion is entirely done by homophony.

Tutorial

Studying Metre

Questions

1. Define the following terms: rhyme, assonance, consonance, onomatopoeia, rhyme scheme, para-rhyme, blank verse.
2. What are the two main effects of homophony?

Discussion Point

Is rhyme now old-fashioned, or can modern poets make interesting use of it? Try to find some examples.

Practical Assignments

1. Compose a short, humorous stanza in each of the following forms: ABAB, AABA, ABBA, ABBACC, ABCDCBA, ABBCDDCAA. Then make up some forms of your own.
2. Look for different kinds of homophony in the world around you, including brand names, newspaper headlines and advertising slogans.

Study Tips

- Remember not to be an anorak: always ask yourself what homophony <u>means</u> once you've spotted it.
- The more poetry you read and analyse the better you'll get at recognising what's unusual and what's common in different periods, and the more you will enjoy poetry.

5 Metaphor

One-minute overview

A metaphor is a 'figure of speech' – an unusual way of saying something. In fact, metaphors are everywhere and being able to analyse them is an essential skill for literary critics.

In a metaphor one thing is compared with another. As well as the classic metaphor, in this chapter we'll look at allegories, analogies, symbols and other figures of speech that compare two different things.

We're now moving away from the purely formal elements of metre and homophony into a more sophisticated area. Metaphor is a formal element, but it's also very closely dependent on the content of the poem. In the previous chapters, we've analysed poetry without too much concern over what the words mean. From here on, the words will be very important indeed.

In this chapter you will learn:
- What is meant by the term 'metaphor'
- How to recognise and analyse metaphors
- What similes, symbols, allegories, analogies and conceits are
- What metaphors can mean.

What is a Metaphor?

In a sentence. A metaphor is a phrase that compares two different things without being completely explicit about it. A metaphor is actually composed of three parts: canon, figure and ground. By learning to analyse these you'll learn to identify and make sense of metaphors.

Metaphor as Comparison and Generalisation

In a metaphor A is compared with B as a way of saying something about A. Let's start with a simple, everyday example: Dave is a student who lives in a dirty, frankly disgusting way. He doesn't keep his room clean or tidy, he doesn't eat well and when he does eat it's usually junk food. The way he eats is unpleasant and his clothes are not often washed. One of the women on his course described Dave by saying 'Dave is a pig'. We'll assume that we know that Dave isn't literally a pig. He's being compared with a pig to explain the nature of his lifestyle in a manner that carries meaning.

Now, conventionally (and this is very unfair on pigs) these creatures have poor manners, particularly in two areas: at the table and in matters of the heart. Let's assume that the context of the phrase tells us that Dave's eating dinner. We already know about his eating habits from the description above. Hence, Dave and the pig are said to be the same in respect of their eating habits.

Yet the phrase simply says that Dave _is_ a pig. This is what a metaphor is and how it works – two things that have one feature in common are said to be identical. The two are compared, but the comparison is generalised.

Simile

A simile is an explicit metaphor. If we'd said, 'Dave eats like a pig', then we'd have used a simile. Similes are easy to analyse because they're explicit, so there's not much more to say.

Some writers claim that if we'd said 'Dave is like a pig', that too would be a simile just because the word 'like' makes it explicit that a comparison is taking place. That may be so, but you still need to do the same analytical work as if it were a metaphor, so why worry about it?

If in doubt, use 'simile' where you see phrases such as 'A is like B' or 'A is as big as a B'. The word 'metaphor', in modern literary criticism, has far wider application than it used to, and 'simile' is used much less, so only the most pedantic of readers will complain if you use 'metaphor' instead of 'simile'.

Canon, Figure and Ground

Dave, the pig and the eating habits that unite them are the three essential parts of this metaphor, and you won't be surprised to learn that there are technical terms for them: canon, figure and ground. Here they are:

Canon	Dave	The one being described
Figure	The pig	The thing used to describe the canon
Ground	The table manners	The thing which the canon and figure share

The ground is the basis for the metaphor. If Dave asked, 'On what grounds are you calling me a pig?' our poet could reply, 'Your filthy eating habits'. You can change the canon or the figure, and you can even change the ground:

Canon	Geraldine is a pig (same figure and ground)
Figure	Dave is a monkey (okay, maybe this is a stretch, but monkeys are pretty messy eaters too)
Ground	Dave was a pig to Geraldine (now we're talking about Dave's romantic behaviour, so the ground has changed)

Here are some more examples:

Example	Canon	Figure	Ground
Sue was left high and dry	Sue	A shipwrecked boat	Both are helpless and abandoned
Pete ratted on his mates	The week	A long road	Necessary, boring task of getting from one end to another

You'll notice that in each case we've found something that isn't said explicitly in the phrase itself: the ground. We might also find that the figure was partly implicit, as in the 'high and dry' example; the phrase doesn't mention a boat at all.

More Complex Metaphors

Poetic metaphors are often more complicated than everyday ones, and this kind of analysis will reveal a fair bit of additional material. For example, here's Shelley on the state of 'England in 1819':

Rulers ... leechlike to their fainting country cling

Here rulers (canon) are compared with leeches (figure). The ground is the parasitic way of life of the leech. The metaphor works especially well because leeches have negative connotations: no one usually likes a leech. As well as being descriptive, Shelley's line is also insulting to the 'rulers'. You'll often find that this is the case; negative figures are used for negative descriptions, and positive ones where the metaphor is supposed to be flattering. Here's the Monty Python team subverting this tradition:

"My Lord is like a stream of bat's piss."

"WHAT?"

"I merely meant, my Lord, that you shine out like a shaft of gold when all around is dark."

If you find inappropriate terms used like this in a serious metaphor, always ask yourself why - there are likely to be valuable clues hiding there.

Shelley's metaphor is connected to a second one, comparing the country (canon) to a person (figure) who the leeches cling to. The ground's harder to find this time, unless you know that it's very common to compare Britain with a human body, with the monarch at the head and the different regions and functions of the country as the different parts of the body, all working together. This was known as the 'body politic' in the Renaissance, and it's an idea we still use today: when we talk about a company being 'corporate' we're using a word derived from the Latin 'corpus', meaning 'body'. Instead of the monarch being the head, the ruler is now a leech on the body: this, as you'll see in the next chapter, is an example of irony.

That's nearly 200 words of analysis, not counting Monty Python, from just eight words of poetry – and we haven't even related this to the rest of the poem yet. As a literary critic a metaphor is a gift to you – if you analyse it carefully.

How Significant is the Metaphor?

This is the question you must always ask yourself. The answer will be, roughly, one of the following three.

Ornamental

Ornamental metaphors are just there to produce a local effect, as the image of the sky as a vault which appears in these lines from Tennyson's '*The Lotos Eaters*':

Hateful is the dark-blue sky

Vaulted o'er the dark-blue sea

Death is the end of life; ah, why

Should life all labor be?

Here the sky is the canon, the vault the figure and the apparently dome-like shape of the sky is the ground. Whenever looking at ornamental metaphors, see whether they are related to the themes that the lines are discussing. Here the infinity of sky and sea beyond the Lotos Eaters' island is invoked to represent death; a vault is another name for a crypt.

Thematically important

Shelley's metaphor of leeches for rulers is an important part of his theme, which is the decline of monarchy and the established order in England. It's only one of several different metaphors in the poem but it's an important one and you'd expect it to link up with the others in an interesting way.

Central

Some metaphors are really central to a poem. In most cases these are too extended to be properly considered metaphors – next we'll talk about allegories and conceits, which are essentially metaphors that have run out of control.

Step-by-Step Analysis

As you start practising analysis of metaphors follow these steps; you'll soon get the hang of it and be able to work in a more instinctive way.

1. Pick out the figure and canon. This should be easy enough.
2. Try to work out what the ground is. This can be more difficult and it might be conventional rather than self-evident.
3. Are the figure, canon and ground unexpected in any way? Are you surprised by any of them?
4. Is the metaphor a cliché like 'Dave is a pig' or is it more unusual?
5. Are there two or three metaphors mixed together? If so, separate them from each other. This is what 'analysis' means, separating and simplifying that which is obscure and complex.
6. If several metaphors are involved, ask yourself what their relationship is.
7. How does the metaphor relate to the poem as a whole?

Extensions of the Metaphor

As we've seen, 'straightforward' metaphors like Tennyson's 'vaulted' sky aren't the only kind. If you're beginning to feel that metaphors like Shelley's leeches can be complicated, confusing and difficult to make complete sense of, you're right.

Metaphor is one of the most important components of language helping to make language as complex and open to interpretation as it is. In this section we'll see how metaphors can get out of hand (that is, we lose control of them) in two different ways. They can be extended to breaking point, where they become 'conceits', or they can be flawed in their construction, when we call them 'mixed metaphors'.

Conceits

Here's a simple definition of a conceit: it's a metaphor in which the figure and the canon are expanded to an extent that they're not simply 'mapped onto' each other any more. In the works of the metaphysical poets like John Donne and Andrew Marvell, a single metaphor is often extended into a conceit that takes up the entire poem.

A conceit tends to be more ambiguous than a straightforward metaphor. In other words, its meaning is less clear, which allows for complex, more-than-meets-the-eye meanings. That, as you know, is good news for you. Here's a couple of examples.

Example 1: Shelley

Shelley's metaphor could be seen as an example of a conceit. Here it is in context:

Rulers who neither see, nor feel, now know,

But leechlike to their fainting country cling

Till they drop, blind in blood, without a blow

Instead of thinking of two metaphors, think of just the one – 'rulers are like leeches, in that they are parasitic' – extended into a whole picture. The ground is now a whole range of qualities: blindness, insensitivity, stupidity, weakness and decadence.

Interestingly – and here's what makes these lines a good candidate for being a conceit – the way the canon and the figure are expanded are quite different. The canon is given a list of qualities: the rulers can't see, feel or know. The figure, though, is given a little narrative: it clings, fills up with blood and then drops off (that is, loses power). It's as if the canon is used for description and the figure provides a sequence of events.

This kind of independent expansion of figure and canon is a distinguishing feature of a conceit. You'll find there's a lot of work to do before you'll have made sense of it, but once you have you'll be in possession of some first-rate essay material.

Example 2: Emerson

Here is another kind of conceit, taking up a whole short poem by Ralph Waldo Emerson called 'Grace':

How much, preventing God! how much I owe

To the defenses thou hast round me set:

Example, custom, fear, occasion slow,

These scorned bondmen were my parapet.

I dare not peep over this parapet

To gauge with glance the roaring gulf below,

The depths of sin to which I had descended,

Had not these me against myself defended.

Again, we should look for the central metaphor, which seems to be comparing God's grace with the walls of a castle, the ground being the protective value each has.

The poem, though, gently turns our expectations on their head. Whereas a castle's parapets are designed to keep an attacking enemy out, it seems that God's spiritual parapets in fact keep the narrator inside, free from temptation and the 'depths of sin'. Again, the canon and figure part company slightly: they've been extended in different directions, and they don't make a straightforward fit any more.

If this poem were first encountered in an 'unseen' exam, one idea would be to look for a problem in this situation, something that makes it less simple than it first appears. For example, look at the last line, which pinpoints the contradiction in the conceit: my castle protects me from you, and my prison protects you from me, but the structure that Emerson describes protects me from myself.

You might notice that the walls of God's grace are described in oddly negative terms:

Example, custom, fear, occasion slow,

These scorned bondmen were my parapet.

Could Emerson be using the ambiguity of the conceit to ask whether 'God's grace' is no more than social taboo, a restriction on personal freedom? Only a more extended analysis could reveal that, but identifying the conceit would be the start of the process.

Mixed Metaphors

A mixed metaphor is one that doesn't make sense. You may have come across it when listening to someone who uses a lot of clichés without thinking about them. They end up saying something like, 'David, stop shovelling your food like a pig.' Here, two metaphors have been blended into one sentence:

David is shovelling his food.

David is a pig.

When we say that someone is shovelling their food, we mean that they are eating like someone digging a hole in the road: ungracefully and with an air of performing a laborious task. The figure is a manual worker, and for David to eat like a manual worker would simply never do in polite English society.

If David is eating like a pig, though, he's unlikely to be shovelling. In fact, if David is eating like a pig then he's eating like an animal, which isn't sophisticated enough to use tools like shovels.

Mixed metaphors are usually contradictory, like this one. It disparages David for using a shovel (metaphorically) and for being like an animal, which can't use utensils. Yet they are also usually revealing. The speaker, without meaning to, has created a third metaphor: 'Manual workers are like animals'. That's quite likely to surprise the person who said it.

This is an example of what modern critical theorists sometimes call 'slippage': the tendency that language has to betray you by slipping out of control. Mixed metaphors and other 'accidental' features are one place where this slippage is often found.

Example: Swinburne

Here's a snippet by Algernon Charles Swinburne from 'The Poet and the Woodlouse', which is anything but accidental:

Man, the fleshy marvel, always feels a certain kind of awe stick

To the skirts of contemplation, cramped with nympholeptic weight;

Don't worry: it's a parody and Swinburne is being deliberately confusing. Nympholepsy is a seizure brought on by an unattainable beauty. Its dictionary definition is 'a frenzy supposed by ancient peoples to have been induced by nymphs' (Houghton Miffin Dictionary of the English Language).

The rest of the words are perfectly understandable, though, so why is it so hard to comprehend what he means?

Well, the lines are plagued by mixed metaphors. The phrase 'skirts of contemplation' seems to be a metaphor along these lines:

Canon	Figure	Ground
Contemplation	Clothing	Being "wrapped up" in one or the other

The idea of being 'wrapped up in contemplation' brings with it an image of staying still. However, the idea that awe 'sticks' to these skirts and weighs them down implies that the contemplator is trying to go somewhere and being hindered. This looks like a second metaphor:

Canon	Figure	Ground
Contemplation	A journey	The intention of reaching a conclusion: a solution to the problem being likened to the destination of a journey

The idea that awe in the face of the majesty of the universe might weigh down the thinker and make it more difficult to understand her subject makes perfect sense. The two different pictures that these two lines try to conjure up – the thinker 'wrapped up in contemplation' and the thinker on a 'journey of discovery' – are both clichés, but to invoke both at once Swinburne uses a mixed metaphor that isn't just unfamiliar, it's very hard to make any sense of at all.

Coupled with his use of obscure words (which gets worse, not better, as the poem goes on) these lines seem foolish and pretentious. The clichés only add to the image of a narrator with little imagination or intelligence disguising the fact by means of over-complicated language.

When a Metaphor isn't a Metaphor

People often get the term 'metaphor' mixed up with terms like 'symbol', 'analogy' and 'allegory'. To make sure you aren't one of those people, here are definitions of those terms and some brief examples.

Symbol

A symbol is commonly defined as an 'overdetermined image' but that isn't very helpful if you don't know what 'overdetermined' means. A symbol is essentially something that has a great deal of different meanings crammed into a single word or phrase.

So it's never advisable to say something like 'Oh, a lion is a symbol of bravery', in a breezy, know-it-all voice. Maybe, in a particular poem, a lion is being used as a figure for a brave person in a metaphor, and bravery is the ground. That would be a more exact way of putting it.

Conventionally, a lion can represent nobility, monarchy, savage nature, Jesus Christ (Most Western European symbols come from the Bible, the Greek classics, medieval art and Renaissance science), Richard III, England and more. For instance, the lion was introduced in Singapore in 1986 as an alternative national symbol. The lion was chosen because they felt it best captured the characteristics of Singapore's reputation as the Lion City.

So the lion is used as a symbol to represent nobility, monarchy, savage nature, Jesus Christ, Richard III, England and Singapore, among other things. The point to understand is that its meaning isn't determined by just one thing: it's overdetermined. The examples given show that it can mean all sorts of different things. Learning these different conventions is something that will come with time; the more you read, the more you'll understand.

Allegory

An allegory is a way of talking about one thing to mean something else. You might imagine talking about a shepherd and his sheep to explain the relationship between God and humanity as a way of making the concepts more immediate and easier to understand. Formally speaking, there are two kinds of allegory: narrative and 'speaking pictures'.

The difference between allegory and metaphor is that an allegory is extended and complex, but the figure is focused on almost exclusively. The reader is usually expected to know what the canon is, perhaps from just a few lines at the beginning or end, and to use her/his imagination to work out how it corresponds to the figure.

Narrative allegory

A narrative allegory is easy to understand: it's a story that follows the same pattern as another story, and it's intended that the reader will find the relationship between the two illuminating. The fall of Satan from heaven, for example, has been used as an allegory within Christianity for human pride and sin. Narrative allegory was a staple of European medieval literature, and although it has never fallen into total disuse, it has become less popular as literature has concerned itself less with moral instruction.

Speaking pictures and 'blazon'

A speaking picture is a technique that was developed during the Renaissance from the medieval practice of 'blazon'. A blazon is a way of saying in words what a heraldic crest looks like, and it proceeds by describing each part very carefully in a prescribed order. Here's Chaucer describing the Wife of Bath:

Her headscarves were very fine in texture;

I dare say there was ten pounds in weight

That she wore on her head on a Sunday.

Her stockings were fine scarlet,

Tied very straight, with soft, new shoes.

Her face was bold, fair and ruddy.

[...]

Gap-toothed she was, truly,

She rode at ease on an ambling horse,

Properly veiled, and on her head was a hat

As broad as a soldier's shield;

A riding skirt was around her large hips,

And on her feet were a pair of sharp spurs.

The Wife of Bath's Prologue and Tale (Cambridge School Chaucer) by Geoffrey Chaucer, Valerie Allen (Editor)

Now, this might look like a straightforward description to you, but look at it again: look at the meticulous detail with which Chaucer described each feature. This is a literary 'blazon', and it's full of significance. He's at pains to tell us what a modest woman she is, with her veil, strait-laced stockings and Sunday-best headscarves, but he mentions a number of things that are at odds with it: her ostentatious hat, wide hips and fair complexion (these last two were both 'sexy' features, at least in Chaucer's time) and rather aggressively sharp spurs.

Chaucer's narrator mentions that she's had five husbands – then suddenly changes direction and talks about her pious pilgrimages instead. The narrator may be shy of the fact, but his description shows her to be a vivacious, unconventional and even outrageous character.

A 'speaking picture' (the phrase is Sir Philip Sidney's, from his 'Apology for Poetry') works in much the same way. It builds up fragments to produce a picture in which the overall meaning depends on the meanings of the different bits and how they are put together. You can spend a lot of time analysing a speaking picture like this, and a knowledge of the poetic conventions and symbols of the time is often essential. Look out for the technique next time you see a description; although it's a typically European Renaissance technique, you can even spot it in modern works now and again.

Analogy

An analogy is to an allegory what a simile is to a metaphor. That is, an analogy is an explicit allegory, in which each part of one thing is mapped explicitly on to another.

Analogies are common in science and technology, but not in poetry. Don't be one of those students who says, 'Oh, the Wife of Bath's physical appearance is an analogy of her moral character'. Wrong: it's a speaking picture or an allegorical description. If it were an analogy, it would be much more explicitly laid out, and each element of the 'canon' would be related to an element in the 'figure'.

Tutorial
Studying Metaphor
Questions

1. Define 'canon', 'figure' and 'ground'.
2. What is a conceit? What is a mixed metaphor?
3. What are symbols, narrative allegories, speaking pictures and analogies? How does each differ from a metaphor?

Discussion Points

- How much metaphor do we use in our daily lives?
- Can we control our language, or are we always in danger of 'slippage'?

Practical Assignments

1. Look out for metaphors in everyday life. Advertisements and common figures of speech are both good places to start.
2. If you have access to children's books, see if any of them have allegorical narratives; many do, especially more old-fashioned ones.

Study Tip
Collect metaphors – whether mentally or on paper – as you read different poems. See which ones are used regularly and which are unusual or even unique.

6 Rhetorical Tropes

One-minute overview

Rhetoric is the art of fine speaking; a trope is a trick, a turn of phrase, a figure of speech that improves your performance as an eloquent speaker or writer. The rules of rhetoric were formulated in ancient Greece but they have long been a part of English poetry. In this chapter we won't be studying formal rhetoric – we'll be looking at how poets actually use it and what effect it has.

Identifying a rhetorical 'trope' in a poem is a useful way into analysing it. Here, we'll look at all the common tropes and a good number of less common ones. We'll also see that rhetoric in general was at the centre of a controversy that has haunted English poetry ever since.

In this chapter you will learn:
- what is meant by the term 'trope'
- what 'rhetoric' means in poetry
- the common tropes of metonymy and synecdoche (sin-eck-DOE-key)
- more exotic tropes and how to analyse them.

What is a Trope?

A trope is a substitution of terms where one term holds a place in a string of words for another, which is usually not present. The four master tropes are metonymy, metaphor synecdoche and irony.

In a metaphor, instead of saying 'Dave is greedy', you say 'Dave is a pig', because it is generally understood that pigs are greedy and (supposedly) disgusting. The trope intensifies your condemnation of Dave by saying that he's greedy and disgusting (and more besides). So a metaphor is a type of trope. There are many other tropes – recipes, if you like, for making a more elegant statement than the straightforward one.

A Brief History of Rhetoric in English Poetry

The poetry that you're likely to be studying will have been written during or after the European Renaissance. Before then, rhetoric was something studied by scholars, alongside logic and grammar. The following brief summary will help you to put rhetoric in context.

The Renaissance...

During the Renaissance, interest in ancient writers like Cicero and Aristotle started to increase. The Elizabethan age saw rhetorical 'devices' highly praised for their ingenuity, neatness and cleverness.

But this is only one aspect of our story. The other important aspect is the Reformation, which began during the 1530s under Henry VIII. Protestantism quickly developed a tradition of 'iconoclasm', which means 'destroying images'. Paintings and sculptures were taken from Catholic churches and burned or smashed on a massive scale; any sign of 'showiness', was eventually seen as superstition.

This tendency (which quickly developed into Puritanism) also carried over into literature, where 'plain speaking' and humble simplicity were considered much godlier than the 'showing-off' of the courtiers. To see the difference between these practices, compare George Herbert's simple verses (although they're more complex than they appear) with Shakespeare's sonnets, which are full of clever turns of phrase.

... and beyond

The conflict between simplicity and rhetoric has been with us ever since. The Romantics favoured a simple approach, more in tune with their rural ideals, while their contemporaries, the Neo-Classicists, looked for formal beauty in complexity. In the early 20th century, Modernists like Ezra Pound wrote densely complicated poetry, while the war poets (like Wilfred Owen) aimed for a simpler, more visceral style.

It's worth bearing this conflict in mind as you study rhetoric in poetry: sometimes you'll find a poet taking one side or the other. Very often, the poet will claim to be using simple, direct speech but in fact employ many rhetorical devices (as Herbert does). This kind of self-referentiality (see below) is going to be valuable to you when you come to write an essay.

Synecdoche and Metonymy

The most common rhetorical tropes are metonymy and synecdoche, which is a kind of metonymy. You'll understand this section better if you've read the 'Canon, Figure and Ground' section of chapter 5, (page 00).

Synecdoche

Synecdoche (pronounced sin-eck-DOE-key) despite being hard to spell, is very, very simple. It means using a physical part to express the whole thing. So the figure (description) is actually a part of the canon (what's described) itself. There's no need for a ground in synecdoche as there is in metaphor, because the two things are already connected.

An example is 'All hands on deck', in which the hands of the crew are used to describe the crew members themselves. After all, if they opened up the hatches and obediently laid just their hands on the deck, the captain would be none too pleased about it.

The thing to look at here is which part is being used. In this example, the crew are reduced to mere hands – the parts that do the work. As far as the speaker is concerned, perhaps they are just units of labour, not people in their own right.

Metonymy

Synecdoche is a kind of metonymy, but metonymy can be broader than just synecdoche. The figure needn't be a physical part of the canon; it could be a quality of it or something associated with it. You could use metonymy to describe a queen using:

- an aspect of the queen, for example 'her Royal Highness'
- an object she is associated with, for example 'the Crown'.

Literary critic David Lodge has remarked that metonymy and synecdoche are much more common in prose, while metaphor is very common in poetry. That's certainly true, but there are examples in poetry, such as Coleridge's 'The ship was cheered' (from 'Rime of the Ancient Mariner'). The ship's crew members were cheered; the ship, which belongs to the crew, is used to refer to them metonymically. If in doubt whether a figure of speech is synecdoche or metonymy, use 'metonymy'.

Other Rhetorical Tropes

In this section, you'll find a list of all of the rhetorical tropes commonly found in English poetry. There are many, many obscure ones, but you won't be expected to see and interpret them; those in this section will give you every one you're likely to need (or want) to know about. Even if you can't pin a name on a trope, the important thing is to be able to see it and analyse it in the context of the poem.

These tropes can be divided into three groups.

- Formal tropes.
- Informal tropes.
- Intertextual tropes.

Formal Tropes

The tropes in this section are concerned with specific uses (or distortions) of grammar, word order or logic. Most are derived from Classical rhetoric.

Chiasmus

Chiasmus means 'crossing over'. Something is first said one way and then said back to front: 'XY, YX'. Sometimes this is done just for effect and sometimes it's used to reverse the meaning. It's usually used, though, to indicate a close binding of the two concepts, as in Shakespeare's line:

Therefore I lie with her and she with me.

Innuendo

Innuendo uses something apparently innocuous to refer to something much more serious and, almost always, something negative. Here's one of Browning's characters, an embittered monk, raising doubts about a fellow monk's virtue:

With Sanchicha, telling stories,

Steeping tresses in the tank,

Blue-black, lustrous, thick as horse-hairs,

– Can't I see his dead eye glow,

Bright as t'were a Barbary corsair's?

Brother Lawrence's excitement over Sanchicha's stories can hardly be said to be a sin, but the innuendo is easy to read – the detailed description of her hair and the gleam in his eye compared with that in a soldier's are the two elements that give away his real interest.

Litotes

To emphasise a positive statement, it can be turned into a negative one by means of litotes, often using 'no'. 'That was a hard game' becomes 'that was no easy game', and so on. The effect is extreme emphasis. It can also be used to soften a very negative judgement too: think of 'she's no rocket scientist' or 'he's no oil painting'.

Meiosis

Sometimes, deliberate understatements are used to draw attention to the scale of the fact being stated. So, 'You could be right' can be an understated way of saying 'Yes, obviously', and the lines of this gospel song aren't to be taken too literally:

What do we think of Jesus?

He's alright.

Oxymoron

Oxymorons are contradictions in terms. They were very popular in the early Renaissance, when English poets imitated Italian writers, especially Petrarch. Here's Sir Philip Sydney commenting on its overuse by fashionable poets of his time:

Some lovers speak when they their Muses entertain

Of hopes begot by fear, of wot not what desires:

Of force of heav'nly beams, infusing hellish pain:

Of living deaths, dear wounds, fair storms and freezing fires.

The last line contains four oxymorons in the strict sense – an adjective (like 'living') that contradicts a noun ('death'). 'Heav'nly beams, infusing hellish pain' is contradictory enough to warrant the term too, as is 'hopes begot by fear', although it might be better to use the more general term 'paradox' for these.

Pun

A pun is a play on words, using one word that sounds like another with the intention that the reader should think of the word that isn't said. If you wanted to sound clever then you could call it an implied homophony.

Rhetorical question

Good public speakers often ask questions that they then answer themselves. It's normally a way of injecting variety into a speech; listening to or reading one thing over an extended period might be a bit dull, but a debate or discussion is much more lively.

Rhetorical questions can seem to come from the narrator, creating an 'internal dialogue', as in this stanza of Herbert's describing the fear of being arrested and executed:

But must they have my brain? Must they dispark

Those sparkling notions, which therein were bred?

Must dullness turn me to a clod?

Yet have they left me, Thou art still my God.

Alternatively, they can be simply an expression of the obviousness of the answer: 'Isn't it better to...?'.

Transferred epithet

In this case, an epithet is a descriptive phrase, and it's transferred from one thing to another. If you received 'an angry letter' it would be the person who wrote it, not the letter, which was really the angry party. Transferred epithets are quite common and they're closely related to metonymy.

The most common effect is that something inanimate (like a letter) seems to behave like a person, or a person seems to behave like an object, as in 'he was a suburban little man', meaning that his house, or his attitudes, were suburban (in a town). It's easy to confuse transferred epithets with metonymy; sometimes a trope will actually be both, sometimes it will just be one or the other.

Informal Tropes

The tropes in this section are looser rhetorical techniques; they are general 'ways of saying things' rather than technical tricks.

Bathos

Bathos means anticlimax or, literally, deflation. A pompous man slipping on a banana skin is bathetic, and the trope is almost always used for comic effect, as in these lines by Swift:

The goddess from her chamber issues

Arrayed in lace, brocades and tissues.

'Tissues' is bathetic because a real goddess would hardly have to worry about blowing her nose. Bathos often uses bodily functions and other staples of slapstick comedy to deflate what seems to be grand, serious poetry.

Apostrophe

Apostrophe is a way of speaking either directly to the audience or, less commonly, to some object or other. Although it isn't like this in the play, the popular image of Hamlet's 'Alas, poor Yorrick' speech being addressed to a skull would be a familiar example.

An apostrophe can give a special quality to the poem, but that quality is likely to be different each time you see it. If Hamlet really did do a speech to a skull, we might see him literally 'staring death in the face' and conversing with it; perhaps the lines would be full of bravado or fear?

Many poems are addressed to God. This is so common that, although it's technically an apostrophe, it's easy to overlook it: don't. Any poem addressed to a specific listener – such as a lover – is a form of apostrophe.

Euphemism

A euphemism is a softer or more acceptable word or phrase than the obvious one. Hence 'doing it' for 'having sexual intercouse', and 'resting' for 'being out of work'; there are hundreds of others in daily use.

Euphemisms can be used out of genuine squeamishness. Alternatively, they can be used ironically, as a form of meiosis (see above); hence 'working girl' for 'prostitute'. Euphemisms can also be deliberately absurd, as in 'vertically challenged' for 'short'.

Euphuism

Not to be confused with euphemism, euphuism is deliberately over-the-top floweriness or otherwise fancy writing. It's usually used as a parody, as in Swinburn's 'The Poet and the Woodlouse'. Here's a whole stanza of pure euphuism (it's the woodlouse talking):

And I sacrifice, a Levite – and I palpitate, a poet;–

Can I close dead ears against the rush and resonance of things?

Symbols in me breathe and flicker up the heights of the heroic

Earth's worst spawn, you said, and cursed me? look! approve me!
I have wings.

The fact that this is euphuism – not just utter madness – is evident from the nicely timed bathos of the last line.

Watch out for the classic mistake of claiming something is euphuistic just because you don't understand it. Make sure it's clearly an effect in the poem; often this will be signalled by elements of absurdity, like the very fact that the poet is talking to a woodlouse in the first place.

Hyperbole

Hyperbole is a clever Greek word for exaggeration. When someone claims that they've told you 'a million times' not to do something, they're probably employing hyperbole. The device was common in Renaissance love poetry and remains so in modern political mud-slinging.

An extreme phrase is usually used because the speaker feels strongly about something, and the words that would accurately describe the situation don't seem up to the job. Hyperbole therefore says more about the narrator's (not the poet's) feelings than about the thing in question.

Irony

'Irony' is a difficult word to define. Essentially it means a reversal, particularly a reversal of the value of something. If someone won the lottery and died of a heart attack as a result of the excitement, you'd say that was ironic. Winning the lottery is supposed to make you happy, but dying is sad, and so the value of the event has been reversed.

This is 'narrative irony' – in other words, ironic things happening. Here's a poem by Blake with a neatly ironic narrative:

I asked a thief to steal me a peach,

He turned up his eyes;

I ask'd a lithe lady to lie her down,

Holy & meek she cries.

As soon as I went

An angel came.

He wink'd at the thief

And smil'd at the dame —

And without one word said

Had a peach from the tree

And still as a maid

Enjoy'd the lady.

Of course, in the third stanza we expect the angel to reward the thief and the lady for refusing to give in to the narrator's temptations. Instead the angel is just as bad, in fact worse, because it is able to get what it wants by using supernatural powers.

You will also come across irony in the way a poem expresses itself. Essentially, this sort of irony is like a gentle and rather understated kind of sarcasm. The idea that the angel is 'still as a maid' (that is, a virgin) while seducing the lady is an example of irony.

Note

You'll occasionally see the term 'dramatic irony' used. This doesn't mean the same thing as other kinds of irony and it's very simple. It describes the situation in which a character on stage is unaware of a crucial fact that the audience knows about. You're unlikely to find dramatic irony used in this way in poetry.

Pathetic fallacy

'Pathos' means 'sympathy'. The 'pathetic fallacy' is a particularly Romantic technique, in which the natural world is described as if it had human characteristics and emotions. Generally it's achieved by means of a metaphor or a transferred epithet; think of 'the raging sea' or 'threatening rainclouds'. The effect is normally that the natural surroundings comment on or reflect whatever else is going on: think of thunderstorms in corny horror movies, in which the very forces of nature seem to close in and threaten the hapless victims. Here is Tennyson, describing the island of the Lotos Eaters:

All around the coast the languid air did swoon,

Breathing like one that hath a weary dream.

Sometimes, in poetry, it's as if the thunderstorm is the whole film, with just a few brief scenes to hint at what it's supposed to reflect. In cases like this, it's often working like an extended metaphor or conceit (see Chapter 5).

Personification

Personification is very like pathetic fallacy, but it works slightly differently. An abstract subject (like death) is turned into a character (like the 'Grim Reaper') to make it easier to say things about that subject. In this sense, personification can be like a miniature allegory (see Chapter 5), or part of a larger allegory. Don't use 'personification' to refer to effects that are actually achieved by means of pathetic fallacy; you're looking for a fully drawn, physical character who is used to represent an abstract idea.

Anthropomorphism

Anthropomorphism is very similar to personification, except that instead of an abstract idea, the subject is an object or animal. Disney films thrive on anthropomorphism, as do many children's stories and poems.

Intertextual Tropes

'Intertextuality' means a relationship between the poem and another text. It names a special set of rhetorical tropes in which many modern literary critics are particularly interested.

In all but the last case, spotting intertextual tropes is dependent on whether you know the other text. For this reason, poems that use them heavily tend not to appear in 'unseen' exams. If it's for coursework, your edition of the poems ought to contain a footnote that will help you; otherwise you may have to do some research in the library.

Literary allusion

Allusions are references to other pieces of writing. These will often be other works of literature. As well as showing the writer's knowledgeability (especially if the work alluded to is an obscure one) it also compliments the intelligence of the reader who understands it. Beyond these simple effects, a literary allusion claims a connection between the poem and the work that is alluded to. What impact that has will depend on both works.

An allusion isn't always direct or explicit. You might not spot it or you might not be able to decipher it. Don't worry; you won't be alone, but the more widely you read the better your chances are of identifying allusions and working out why they're there.

Quotation

The fact that a poem contains a quotation won't always be obvious. 'The Waste Land' is full of quotations, but if you didn't know where they came from you could easily assume that T.S. Eliot had written them himself. Like allusion, the effect of quotation depends completely on what has been quoted; often, though, you'll find books quoted as authorities, used to back up the narrator's argument. In that case the quotation will often, but not always, come from the Bible or the Greek or Latin Classics.

Parody

To parody something means to imitate it in order to reveal its inherent absurdities. There are plenty of examples of parody in Pope's writings (you'll find a few in this book). It should be obvious when you see it; again, if you've read enough, you'll understand what's being parodied. If not, you'll have some difficulties. Normally, though, a poem will parody a whole style or school of writing rather than an individual, and so a basic, broad knowledge will usually see you through.

Self-referentiality

This final element of intertextuality is the result of a poem referring to itself. Sometimes this is done explicitly, and then it's likely to be an important theme. For example, many Renaissance poems claim that they will outlive their author and so make him, his ideas or the subject of his poem (usually a lover) immortal.

Some literary critics claim that all poetry is self-referential, and that analysis can show that writing is a theme of every single poem. That may be an exaggeration, but not much of one. You should always be on the lookout for hints that a poem is asking questions about writing, poetry, language, communication or meaning – even if its theme seems to be something completely different. There are always points to be scored from spotting self-referentiality in a poem that isn't obviously about itself.

Tutorial

Studying Rhetorical Tropes

Questions

1. Define the following terms:
a) Rhetoric
b) Trope
c) Oxymoron
d) Transferred epithet
e) Apostrophe
f) Hyperbole
g) Irony
h) Pathetic fallacy.

2. Explain the difference between:
a) metonymy and synecdoche.
b) innuendoes and puns.
c) litotes and meiosis.
d) euphemism and euphuism.
e) bathos and pathos.
f) personification and anthropomorphism.

Discussion Points

- Why do people use rhetoric? Is it more honest to avoid it?
- Is a poem a work of art if it doesn't use any rhetoric at all?

Practical Assignment

Come up with your own examples of each rhetorical trope, either in poetic or prose form.

Study Tips

- Don't try to memorise all these terms now – use this chapter for reference, and whenever you think you've seen a trope that's defined here, have a look. Eventually, they'll stick in your mind.
- The most important thing, isn't to remember the terms, it's to get familiar with this way of analysing poems. Eventually if you come across a trope that isn't exactly like one of those defined here, you'll have the confidence to analyse it for yourself.

7   Genre and Style

One-minute overview

'Genre' and 'style' both describe the way a poem is written. 'Genre' describes the broad category that the poem fits into, and is often quite formal. 'Style' deals more with the 'feel' of the writing, and can be quite individual to a poet or even a particular poem.

After the hard analytical material in the preceding chapters, this will probably seem quite straightforward. Armed with these newly acquired skills you'll be in a better position to say something constructive about genre and style.

In this chapter you will learn:

■ what is meant by the terms genre and style

■ the main genres of English poetry

■ the most common styles and how to identify them.

What are Genre and Style?

Genre and style are rarely much use as analytical points because they're too vague and they're not formal enough to give you anything solid. What they can do is give you a 'way in' to a poem, a way of approaching it and starting to think about what it's doing. Knowing about genre and style is particularly useful in 'unseen' exams, but it will be of value to you however you study poetry. Note that these categories are based on British and American poetry, although they're applicable in many cases throughout Europe.

Genre

Think of Hollywood movies. You probably already know a lot about genre in that area. Film genres are broad categories like disaster films, romances, epics, thrillers, action movies, comedies and science fiction films. There are also films that don't really fit into any of these categories – they're often thought of as 'art' films or 'experimental' films, like Lynch's *Blue Velvet* or Cronenberg's *Naked Lunch*.

Genres are loose, flexible categories that affect both content and form. An action film will have a certain type of subject matter (content) such as simple, moral conflicts that are resolved through violent action. It will also have some or all of a range of formal features like chase sequences, fights, an overall 'fast pace' and a single narrative thread (often with a romantic sub plot).

Not all action movies fulfill all these requirements. James Bond films, and the *Die Hard* series are examples of films that fit the bill very closely. Tarantino's Pulp Fiction, though, has all the formal features without the moral conflict that traditionally lies at the heart of an action movie. Indeed, the term 'generic' often means 'unimaginative', and using genre conventions loosely is a skill that only more experienced directors can usually employ effectively.

When you're looking at genre in poetry, you'll likewise only find vague guidelines or rules of thumb that give you an idea of the kind of poem that you're looking at.

Style

If 'genre' is a vague term, 'style' is even vaguer. It describes the way a poem is written. Think about films again. Ridley Scott's *Alien* and Paul Verhoven's *Starship Troopers* are both films in the 'science fiction' genre but done in very different styles.

Scott makes *Alien* into a murky, slow-paced film peopled by quite realistic characters, using techniques from the horror genre and the 'fly-on-the-wall' documentary. *Starship Troopers*, however, is a slick, glossy film that borrows heavily from war films and 1980s teen movies. The characters are deliberately two-dimensional and the dialogue is stilted and full of clichés.

These films are within the same genre but have radically different styles – styles that we, as cinema-literate viewers, can immediately recognise even if we can't put names to them.

Some Common Genres in English Poetry

Epic

The epic is one of the earliest genres in English poetry. If something is written in epic form, it is done on a grand scale; it is about big, important events that are often either historical or based on legend. Epic poems take the form of a narrative (story), often about a single person or place. They're usually in a simple metrical form because they're always very long – if it doesn't take up a whole book, it probably isn't an epic.

Examples of epic poems include Homer's *Iliad*, about the siege of Troy; Dante's *Divine Comedy*, about his journey through Hell, Purgatory and Heaven; and Milton's *Paradise Lost*, about the expulsion of Adam and Eve from the Garden of Eden.

Epics tend to be older poems; from around the 17th century interest in writing epics waned and even the long poems began to have different subjects and concerns.

Ballad

A ballad is similar to an epic. Ballads are not as long as epics, but they're written in simple metrical form and some deal with great affairs such as kings and legendary figures. They can also concern themselves with more ordinary people. The older ballads were originally memorised and transmitted orally; they typically tell simple stories and, like modern journalism, they often avoid making moral judgements or comments.

'Ballad form' is a term used to describe the metrical form that was most popular for ballads. This consists of four-line stanzas (called 'quatrains'), usually rhyming ABBA, ABAB or ABCB. The rhythm is typically what's called 'eights and sixes', meaning that it alternates tetrameter and trimeter in iambs or trochees. Here's an iambic example:

| u / | u / | u / | u / |

The wind doth blow today, my love,

...u | u / | u / | u / |

And a few small drops of rain;

| u / | u / | u / | u / |

I never had but one true love,

| u / | | / u | u / |

In cold grave she was lain.

The regularity of rhythms is typical of a ballad stanza, and so is the rather maudlin subject matter. Notice how the reversion of the second syllable in the last line puts a strong emphasis on 'grave' (by creating a caesura after it), a very useful technique if the poem were being read aloud, since it's important for the audience to grasp the fact that the narrator's 'one true love' is dead.

When analysing a ballad, decide whether it is trying to make a moral point or, as is more common, just telling the story 'straight'. If the latter, see if you can find any judgements hiding in the way it's told. People didn't tell these stories for no reason: they were relevant to the way they lived and often referred to attitudes or events that the ballad doesn't even mention. You won't usually be able to work out the details for yourself but you can get a flavour for the judgements that go with them.

Elegy

An elegy is a poem about someone who's died or, by extension, a poem that is about death. Any poem that describes itself as 'in memoriam' (in memory of) someone is an elegy, and many elegies helpfully have the word 'elegy' in their title.

An elegy typically takes the form of a poem about someone who has died recently, normally a friend of the poet. It will contain information about that person – wholly positive, of course. This part of an elegy isn't much different from an obituary in a newspaper. However, the crucial difference is that a poetic elegy expands on this individual death to meditate on death and mortality in general, and it's here that you'll start to find interesting things to say. Tennyson's very long 'In Memoriam' is an example and so is Milton's more manageable 'Lycidas'.

Some elegies, just like action movies, don't fulfil their generic rules entirely; Gray's 'Elegy Written in a Country Churchyard', for instance, dispenses with an individual death and goes straight on to ponder death itself. Other poems may be vaguely about death but you might not want to call them elegies exactly; in that case you can describe them as being 'elegiac', which means 'elegy-like'.

Ode

'Ode' is the hardest word to define in English poetry. It's derived from Greek, but the Greek meaning isn't relevant to English poetry as it was exclusively a dramatic technique.

An ode is like an elegy but it isn't about death. It's a poem that starts out being about something specific (and often fairly trivial) and develops into something more profound. Keats was fond of writing odes, taking things like a nightingale or a Grecian urn and turning them into reflections on the beauty of life.

Use the word 'ode' if the poet does; otherwise, you may want to avoid it. Note that Gray's poem about the death of his cat is called an ode, not an elegy; the elegy was a form of high, serious poetry and to write an elegy about a cat might have seemed rather impertinent.

Sonnet

A sonnet is something you can immerse yourself in as a critic: and if you're studying English poetry you'll get many opportunities, because nearly every poet has written at least one or two.

All sonnets have 14 lines, and there are three kinds:

- Petrarchan
- Shakespearean
- 'other'.

A sonnet is short and pithy, and it involves a twist in the meaning that often gives it an unexpected shift; this part is called the 'turn'. Sonnets are very often in iambic pentameter, but please remember that this is not always the case.

Traditionally, sonnets have been romantic; when an Elizabethan gentleman wrote love poems to his lady they probably would have been sonnets. That association has stayed with us but, in the centuries since Shakespeare, sonnets have been written on all kinds of subjects. They should always be clever and, if it's appropriate, witty. The sonnet was originally a fairly light form of verse, certainly not suited to writing elegies or epics (it's too short, anyway).

Petrarchan sonnets

A Petrarchan sonnet is divided into two sections: first eight lines, then six lines; the turn happens in the middle. Petrarch was an Italian poet who pioneered the sonnet form and made it popular throughout Europe. These sonnets are often printed with a blank line between the two sections, which are called the 'octave' (eight lines) and the 'sestina' (six lines). Here's one of Milton's poems about losing his sight (instead of a blank line, this version uses indentations):

When I consider how my light is spent

Ere half my days, in this dark world and wide,

And that one talent which is death to hide

Lodged with me useless, though my soul more bent

To serve therewith my maker, and present

My true account, lest he returning chide;

"Doth God exact day-labour, light denied?"

I fondly ask; but Patience to prevent

That murmur, soon replies, "God doth not need

Either man's work or his own gifts; who best

Bear his mild yoke, they serve him best. His state

Is kingly. Thousands at his bidding speed

And post o'er land and ocean without rest:

They also serve who only stand and wait."

The octave describes Milton trying to continue writing, as he knows it's a sin to waste his God-given talent, but complaining that God has made it much more difficult by making him blind. In the sestina, however, Patience is personified and explains to him that the inner, spiritual life is the most important and that his outer works are secondary. So, the sestina contradicts the octave, as in the octave the poet is complaining about God and in the sestina he gets his answer.

Notice the 'enjambment' between lines eight and nine (enjambment is the effect of running a sentence across two or more lines). It has two effects; first, it makes the sentence feel fragmented and second, it creates a sense of formal continuity between the lines themselves. In this case it seems designed to give some continuity to the two sections of the poem. The way the octave divides into two groups of four lines, and the sestina into two groups of three is frequently done.

Shakespearean sonnets

The Shakespearean sonnet is exactly like the Petrarchan version, except that the turn only comes between lines 12 and 13. In effect, this means there are three groups of four-line units (usually rhyming ABAB), and then a rhyming 'couplet' (pair of lines) at the end. In the Shakespearean sonnet the turn is less of a dramatic change and more of a summing up of what's gone before:

When I do count the clock that tells the time,

And see the brave day sunk in hideous night;

When I behold the violet past prime,

And sable curls, all silvered o'er with white;

When lofty trees I see barren of leaves

Which erst from heat did canopy the herd

And summer's green all girdled up in sheaves,

Borne on the bier with white and bristly beard,

Then of thy beauty do I question make,

That thou among the wastes of time must go,

Since sweets and beauties do themselves forsake

And dies as fast as they see others grow;

And nothing 'gainst time's scythe can make defense

Save breed, to brave him when he takes thee hence.

Here the first quatrain (four lines) describes the cycle of nature turning from life to death; the second takes the same subject, but transforms it into the image of an old man's funeral. The third quatrain refers to the woman to whom the poem is addressed, explaining how her beauty too must eventually pass away. The final couplet (this is what's called an 'heroic couplet', a self-contained, rhyming pair of lines) makes the general point that the only way to cheat death is to have children ('breed') who will outlive you.

This has quite a twist: in fact it almost has two turns. The hangover from Petrarch can still be felt in the dramatic change from the second quatrain to the third (equivalent of the change from octave to sestina). The final couplet, though, reveals that this is not an elegiac poem about the way that all things wither and turn to dust: it's a 16th-century chat-up line. We can't beat death alone so we'd better make babies instead.

Other kinds of sonnets

If a poem has 14 lines, all of about the same length, and it has a 'twist' or 'turn' somewhere, you're probably justified in calling it a sonnet. There have been all kinds of sonnets written, with lots of variations.

There have even been poems written with more or less than 14 lines, but claiming to be 'sonnets'. If something says it's a sonnet, fine, you can look at which features it shares with traditional forms and which it doesn't. Otherwise, the only one you really need to be aware of is Gerard Manley Hopkins' 'curtal' sonnet, which has six lines, a turn and then four and a half ('God's Grandeur' is an example). Only Hopkins used the form.

Lyric

Now we're back in vaguer territory again. Of course, you already know what lyrics are: the words to a song. And that's exactly what 'lyric' means in poetry: a poem that was originally set to music or, in later pieces, a poem that has a lyrical quality.

Ah, there's the problem. What's a 'lyrical quality'? Truth is, the phrase doesn't mean much. A poem that is properly described as a 'lyric' has the following features:

- Regular metre, but often variable stanza-lengths.
- A rhyme scheme of some sort.
- Subject: love, or some trivial matter (not death or religion). It is not usually a story.
- Content often focuses on the narrator's emotional response to the subject.
- Often a chorus or 'refrain' – repeated line or lines.

A lyric and an ode are therefore quite similar: in fact, an ode is often said to be an example of lyric poetry. As you can see, 'lyric' is a very loose term that you may prefer not to use unless the poet does.

The Very Short Poem

Very short poems are interesting. You can see the whole thing in a single glance and the challenge is to read the details closely enough to be able to write a whole essay on it. Because they have so few words in them they tend to be 'elliptical', meaning that they imply and suggest rather than saying outright.

Epitaphs

There was (and still is, to some extent) a tradition of poets writing epitaphs for other poets who they admired. Since they're supposed to be like carvings on gravestones, even if they weren't actually used for that purpose, they tend to be short. Here's Herrick, 'Upon Ben Jonson':

Here lies Jonson with the rest

Of the poets; but the best.

Reader, would'st thou more have known?

Ask his story, not this stone.

That will speak what this can't tell

Of his glory. So farewell.

It's a typical example. Don't call epitaphs 'elegiac': it's obvious they're about death and they aren't long enough to develop into meditations on death the way that elegies do. In fact, this one picks up on a common theme in Elizabethan poetry – the writer's attempt to make himself immortal by means of his writing.

Limericks

Another short form is the limerick, which is a humorous poem rhyming AABBA, with three long lines and two short ones. As in this example from Edward Lear, the acknowledged master of the form, short lines are sometimes run together:

There was an Old Man with a beard,

Who said, "It is just as I feared! –

Two Owls and a Hen, four Larks and a Wren,

Have all built their nests in my beard!"

Metrically, limericks are actually rather complicated, as you'll find if you analyse this example, but they almost always have the same metrical structure.

Epigrams and other forms

There are many other short poems that don't fit either the epitaph or limerick genre. One such is the 'epigram', a single heroic couplet (two rhyming lines) with a simple, often witty message. Here's Alexander Pope:

Nature, and Newton's laws, lay hid in sight;

God said 'Let Newton be!' and all was light.

You'll find similar pithy, short observations in other metrical forms; you can call them 'epigrammatic'.

The short form is particularly popular with 20th-century poets and the ancient Japanese art of haiku (14 syllables spread over three lines) was revived by the Modernists. The trick is to always ask yourself first: is this a witty little joke or a delicate, suggestive poem?

Complaints and Apologies

You may occasionally come across poems with the word 'complaint' or 'apology' in the title. A 'complaint' was a medieval poem that was characterised by a lot of moaning about how lousy or bad life is, usually because of unrequited love. Like an ode or an elegy, a decent complaint expands on its subject to cover something supposedly universal or at least not something personal. The word fell into disuse after the 16th century.

An 'apology', on the other hand, isn't quite what it sounds like; it's usually a defence or an argument in favour of something that is unfashionable at the time of writing. It's another term that hasn't really been used since the Renaissance (*apologia* is another one of those Greek words they liked so much). A modern example is Geoffrey Hill's deliberately nostalgic 'An Apology for the Revival of Christian Architecture in England'.

Some Common Styles in English Poetry

There are more styles than can possibly be listed in a book like this, but these are some of the most important ones you're likely to come across.

Pastoral

"Pastoral" refers to a romantic image of the countryside, such as shepherds idly playing pipes and gazing at their sheep. An alternative word is 'bucolic', which refers particularly to shepherds, who seem to be big in pastoral poetry. Anything about an idyllic, slow-paced rural life that doesn't mention any of the grubby bits or the hard work that farming really involves, is pastoral.

The pastoral style was popular in the Renaissance (see Spenser's long 'The Shepherd's Calendar') but it had resurgence in the Romantic period – Blake's poem 'The Shepherd', which we saw in Chapter 1, is an example. Its deliberately crude structure and use of simple words presumably indicates the way in which city-dwelling poets thought rural folk spoke; the pastoral can be quite patronising in that way.

The modern versions of pastoral are naivety and primitivism. The latter term refers to the early 20th-century tendency to re-evaluate the works of other cultures (the so-called 'primitives') and to borrow ideas from their work. Naivety, on the other hand, tends to be a reaction against contemporary 'cleverness', a desire for simple and direct expression. A poem can contain a single line that is deliberately naïve; the effect is often bathos (see Chapter 6).

Romanticism

Romanticism is one of the big ones – a movement that lasted from about 1780 to about 1830 and took in Blake, Wordsworth, Byron, Keats, Shelley and Coleridge, along with many lesser-known writers. These are the key features of Romantic poetry (notice the capital 'R', to distinguish it from the 'romantic' fiction of the Mills and Boon variety).

- Hostility towards 'establishment' institutions like the Church of England and the monarchy.
- Emotion and individual feelings are seen as more important than reason and moral rules.
- Unconscious experiences (like dreams) are explored with more interest than ever before.
- Reverence of nature: 'new age'-style mysticism about natural forces, and strong anti-technology tendency. This is more sophisticated than in the pastoral style.

You need to be aware that Romanticism was inspired by German philosophy, especially the work of Schiller and Schlegel. They claimed that there was a strong antagonism between:

This is clearly over-simplified nonsense. But you can use it as your way into Romantic poetry: look to see how the poet tries

Romantic art	Classical art
Emotion	Reason
Nature	Technology
Self-expression	Formal invention
Passion	Calm

to establish a Romantic way of writing and look for the ways this doesn't work out. The best example would be complex formal patterns or use of rhetorical tropes. Your aim isn't to prove Romanticism wrong – it's to show that any particular poem is more interesting than this sort of diagram makes it sound because it's more complex and ambiguous.

Neo-Classicism

Neo-classicism was the other side of the coin to Romanticism. The Neo-classical style was influential on poets from the Augustans like Pope and Dryden through to Victorians like Swinburne and (to a lesser extent) beyond. In each case the writer has taken the formal styles of certain ancient Latin poets and applied it to English poetry in an attempt to create work that is rational, serene and that will stand the test of time.

There are some typical characteristics of the neo-classicist style:

- 'Allusions' that link the poem with the Classical tradition.
- Complex formal schemes.
- Avoidance of personal feelings.

Again, the thing to look for is the way the poem turns out to be interesting despite these neat little theories – the way, for example, formal complexity gets out of control or the way Romantic ideas about nature and poetic inspiration lurk in the background.

Vernacular

The vernacular or 'dialect' style runs from the poems of Robbie Burns right through to contemporary black American writing. Anything that uses obscure slang and/or dialect features like non-standard pronunciations could be described as 'vernacular'. Actually, 'vernacular' means 'of the common people', so you might prefer to use 'dialect' instead. To be really trendy, you could use the term 'ebonics' for black American dialect poetry, although it's not a term that is liked by everyone.

You might find dialect poems difficult to understand. Try – in your head – to adopt the right accent: this often helps.

Impressionism

A term taken from painting, impressionism in poetry is essentially an extension of Romanticism. You may like to use the term wherever a poem aims to describe what it's like to experience an object rather than just what the object is. The technique in painting is very unrealistic; paintings by Monet, for example, don't look anything like photographs, but they try to capture the impression of light and colour on the eye.

Nature poems often use this style. Gerard Manley Hopkins wrote much that could be called 'impressionistic'; here he is describing a bird in flight:

I caught this morning morning's minion, king-

dom of daylight's dauphin, dapple-dawn-drawn Falcon, in his riding

Of the rolling level underneath him steady air

'I saw a bird this morning' would be clear and accurate; Hopkins opts for trying to create an impression of the bird's flight and, especially, the movement of the air instead. Often, you won't be asking yourself, 'Is it impressionism or is it Romanticism?' because it will be both.

Surrealism

A 20th century movement, surrealists were influenced by Freud's theory of psychoanalysis, and particularly his 'discovery' of the subconscious, a dark area of the mind that is normally closed off, but which comes to the surface when the conscious mind loses control – typically when you're asleep.

Surrealists aimed to use symbols in the same way that dreams do: symbols that mean very little on the surface but that can trigger associations in the reader. Avoid saying a particular line or image is 'surreal': use 'surrealist', and only use it if you're pretty sure that the poem as a whole works this way. Some students are easily tempted to describe unusual metaphors or ideas as 'surreal': don't be one of them.

If you find yourself studying a number of surrealist poems, read something introductory on Freud and also Jung; it will help you talk intelligently about the subject.

Modernism and Vorticism

If you're studying English poetry you'll find it hard to avoid modernism, and quite rightly so. A few of the most important modernist poets are Ezra Pound, T.S. Eliot and Sylvia Plath. There are the key features of the modernist style:

- Probably written between 1890 and 1920.
- Free verse (no regular metrical structure).
- No regular rhyme scheme.
- Very intellectual; aimed at highly-educated readers.
- The subject is often the decline of civilisation, the loss of religion and even the 'death' of poetry itself.
- Surrealist techniques were used by many modernist writers; others preferred to plunder older works for quotations, allusions and so on.

Modernism was experimental poetry and thought of itself as on the 'cutting edge' of European literature. It therefore thought that only a small minority would be able to understand it. It was often accompanied by the attitude that everything old should be discarded and poetry be re-made completely new. The result, it was hoped, would be a completely new, pure poetic style.

'Vorticism' was a movement within modernism that especially prized modern technology; it celebrated cities, cars, trains and even mechanised warfare. Vorticists loved the energy and power of the modern world and saw in it a hope that Europe would progress beyond the stagnation that they saw at the end of the 19th century. Some modernist poets sympathised with the Nazi movement, which likewise prized technology and progress. During early modernism, of course, Hitler was still painting houses, although a continuing attachment to Nazism as the century progressed becomes difficult to excuse. Vorticism was a very important force in modernism; take a look at Wyndham Lewis' writings for some examples.

You'll have noticed that modernism is defined as much by content as by form. In that sense it's halfway to being a genre rather than a style. You could write an elegy in a modernist style but you'd be hard pushed to manage a ballad, and a limerick would be pretty much impossible.

Postmodernism

The term 'postmodernism' started being applied to literature around the early 1970s, and people still use it today. Instead of chasing after modernist purity (think of all those big geometrical paintings, or the concrete cubes that modernist architects excitedly built in the 1940s), postmodernists tend to say, 'Anything goes'.

Actually, it's not as simple as that. Postmodern poems use a 'collage' of different poetic styles, mixing up, say, traditional metrical systems, free verse and even prose in a single piece of writing. Next time you're in a city centre, take a look at a big, recently built shopping mall. They often use a variety of architectural styles such as corporate glass and steel, gothic window frames and Victorian industrial girders. That's one aspect of postmodernism: all styles become possible.

Postmodernists tend to be a cheerful lot. Instead of worrying about atheism and the decline of civilisation (like modernists), they celebrate the wide range of different styles and techniques that become available to you if you don't dedicate yourself to any one in particular. In postmodernist writing you'll find a lot of pastiche (parody), kitsch (deliberate cheesiness) and so on. Of course, all these techniques have been used in other kinds of poetry, so for safety you should only use the term for poems written in this style after about 1970.

Tutorial

Studying Style and Genre

Questions

1. What is style? What is genre? What's the difference?
2. Define the following terms:

   a) Epic

   b) Ballad

   c) Elegy

   d) Ode

   e) Lyric

   f) Epitaph

   g) Epigram.
3. Define a sonnet and explain the differences between the Petrarchan and Shakespearean versions.

Discussion Points

- Do poets always write in an identifiable style, or are some poems completely idiosyncratic – that is, unlike any other in terms of style? Make sure you refer to examples in your discussion.
- Are poems written without any genre usually more interesting than 'generic' ones, or does the genre enable the poet to do something complex within it? Use examples and be specific.

Practical Assignment

Many of the names of different poetic styles also apply to styles of painting. Take a trip around a large art gallery and look for examples of pastoral, Romantic, neo-classical, impressionist, surrealist, naive, primitivist, modernist, vorticist and postmodernist painting. Tagging along with a guided tour can be very helpful, and your resulting knowledge will really help you to grasp what these terms mean.

Study Tips

- Find anthologies of poetry in each style (some will be easier to find than others) and quickly read through them to get a 'feel' for the style in question. You'll only get this by reading large amounts, but you don't have to study everything in detail. This will pay big dividends if you have to sit 'unseen' exams.
- Remember, always look for what effect a genre or style has on the meaning of a poem. It's not much use to simply observe that it's a Romantic elegy; use this as a 'way in' to the poem.

8 ▮ Structural Analysis

One-minute overview

For half a century 'Structuralism' was a major force in literary criticism. Since the 1960s it has become less fashionable, but it has provided some very useful techniques for analysing poetry in a completely fresh way.

Structural analysis focuses on the content but treats it formally. That might seem rather obscure now, but all will become clear as we work through this chapter. There are two basic kinds of structure: narrative structure and thematic structure. We'll look in detail at thematic structure because this is more applicable to poetry.

In this chapter you will learn:
- what is meant by the term 'structuralism'
- how to analyse thematic structure
- how to use structuralist techniques in your own analyses.

What is Structuralism?

'Structure' can mean all kinds of things in literary criticism but since the 1950s there's been an extra meaning that is quite technical. Let's take a moment to look at the background to this. It is a bit obscure and a handful of paragraphs is nowhere near enough to get to the bottom of it. Still, hopefully you'll get a flavour of what structural analysis is all about.

Language

Ferdinand de Saussure's *Course in General Linguistics* shook the world. It's a structural account of how language produces meaning out of sounds or marks on bits of paper. It wasn't the first, but it's by far the most influential.

Saussure argued that a word doesn't mean anything by itself. The word 'green', for example, doesn't have anything inherently green about it. A word only has a meaning because it's a part of a whole language, and a language is a kind of system, or structure.

So, 'green' has meaning in relation to other words. 'Green' really means 'the colour in between yellow and blue in the spectrum'. And, you guessed it, 'yellow' and 'blue' have similar meanings. In other words, all meaning is relative to other words.

After all, if someone asked you to define 'green', how would you do it? You'd use other words, wouldn't you? You could point to something green and hope they got the right idea, but that's not the point: it seems like the most natural thing in the world to define words using other words, and that's because this is how they really get their meanings.

So in summary, a word gets its meaning from the place it occupies in the overall structure of a sentence.

Myths

Anthropologist Claude Lévi-Strauss picked up on de Saussure's ideas and tried to apply them to the study of myths and legends. The result – the three-volume *The Raw and the Cooked* (University of Chicago Press), a masterpiece of 20th-century academic writing.

Lévi-Strauss took mythic stories and broke them down into their main components. He then treated them exactly the way de Saussure treated the words in a language: as if the myth as a whole were a structure and each part of the myth only gained meaning in relation to the other parts.

Everything Else...

That might sound like an intellectual exercise, but the results are impressive and they inspired literary critics to try the same thing. Virtually every branch of the Humanities and the Social Sciences at one time or another picked up structuralism, but it's now been abandoned by almost all of them. The main problem is that things just don't seem to work that way. The world isn't really a closed, static structure that can be mapped out.

What's been left over, though, is something very useful: a whole set of techniques and ideas that you can use in your own analyses. You don't have to understand structural linguistics or anthropology to use these techniques – you just need to know how they work.

A Word of Warning

Structural analysis is a powerful tool. Use it with care. Avoid anything that isn't justified by the words on the page. It's easy to get carried away and start analysing structures instead of poems. Don't do that: your readers will spot it a mile off and won't be impressed.

Binary Oppositions

In any kind of structural analysis, 'binary oppositions' are central. A poem invariably contains many binary oppositions and being able to analyse them will often prove extremely helpful, even if you don't take your structural analysis any further than that.

What is a Binary Opposition?

A binary opposition is a pair of terms that are opposites. It's a loose definition. All of these examples are binary oppositions, even though some are 'opposite' in quite different ways from others:

Black	White
True	False
Man	Woman
Life	Death
Rich	Poor
Poetry	Prose

For example, you can be halfway between black and white but not between man and woman. A story could be partly true and partly false but a person could hardly be partly rich and partly poor. None of these differences matters: just because these are pairs of terms that we think of as opposites, they're binary oppositions.

Binary oppositions can be neatly written down like this: good/evil. That's the way you'll find them written in this chapter.

What kinds of things can be opposed?

Binary oppositions don't have to contain abstract terms; they can just as easily contain objects or even people, as in these examples:

God	Devil
Mother	Father
Man	God

Notice that 'God' appears twice; just because x is the opposite of y, that doesn't stop it being the opposite of z as well. In a poem about God fighting Satan, the opposition will be God/Satan, but in a poem about man confronting God, the opposition will be man/God.

An 'opposition' doesn't have to be an antagonistic relationship. They just have to have opposite meanings, or opposite elements of their meanings. So mother/father is an opposition because mother is female and father is male, even though they're hardly opposites like black/white, and they share some features in common (like being human parents, at least, though one would hope they have more in common than that).

Privilege

It's extremely common for the two terms in an opposition to be unequal. One will often be thought of as superior to the other in some important way. When that happens we say that one side of the opposition has been privileged over the other.

This can happen in two ways. The poem itself might privilege one term but, more often, it will simply be traditional. In the opposition good/evil, good is normally privileged. In day/night, the privilege might come on either side; the night could be privileged in a poem about romance, for example, or the day in a poem about searching for the truth (because the light of day is useful when trying to find something).

You'll see more examples of privilege in the next section so don't panic if it's not clear to you just yet.

Identifying Oppositions

Let's look first at some simple binary oppositions in this short poem by W.S. Landor:

I strove with none, for none was worth my strife:

Nature I loved, and, next to Nature, Art:

I warmed both hands before the fire of Life;

It sinks; and I am ready to depart.

The title is 'Dying Speech of an Old Philosopher' and so 'depart' in the last line refers to death. Since we have 'Life' at the end of line three, we can identify life/death as an opposition right away.

Nature/art is also present. Although the narrator loved both, the poem makes a clear distinction between the two. Art is artificial and nature is natural and that's the most likely basis for the opposition. Note that the poem privileges nature over art; you'll find quite the opposite happening in some poems.

How about the first line? 'I strove with none' is ambiguous – that is, it could mean one of two things. It might mean that the narrator didn't struggle against anyone, or it might mean that the narrator struggled alone. Either way, we can mark up alone/social onto our list of oppositions, which is starting to look pretty impressive. You can also add striving/not striving and worthy/unworthy, again from the first line.

Analysing Oppositions

When analysing the structure of a poem you can use these three steps:

1. Find a core group of oppositions.
2. Identify the details that don't fit with this simple structure.
3. Work out a complete structure that accounts for all those messy details.

Find a core group of oppositions

Binary oppositions tend to 'line up', which simply means that they go together. This gives you one of the most straightforward ways to analyse them.

Look at these oppositions from the Landor poem:

Alone	Social
Not striving	Striving
Worthy	Unworthy
Philosopher	Others

The column on the left contains the privileged terms; they're the terms that apply to the narrator. When you put the oppositions together like this it gives you part of the picture that the poem is painting.

Another result of this 'lining up' process is that you might easily find additional oppositions hiding in the poem. Look at the philosopher, sitting alone warming 'both hands before the fire', refusing to engage with the strivings of the social world. This is an opposition between leisure and work, subjects that are not mentioned by name anywhere in the poem.

Because the poem is about how the narrator has lived, one might even say that the opposition is one relating to lifestyles rather than just activities. In other words, the poem contains the opposition aristocratic/proletarian (or 'working class'), in which the aristocratic lifestyle is privileged.

Identify the details

We've now got a series of binary oppositions that, we think, add up to the core of the poem's structure. But we also have some other, sticky oppositions that don't fit this structure – yet. Structuralism is about accounting for every little detail and, as you already know, details are usually more revealing than generalisations.

We identified nature/art as an opposition, and it's clearly an important one because it takes up a quarter of the whole poem. But it won't line up with our others because the narrator loved both. We also had life/death, which apply equally to both sides of the core structure. Obviously, our core of oppositions isn't sophisticated enough to cope with these details.

Life and death are both natural, but things are a bit more complicated than that. The poem is about 'Life' (capital 'L'): the worthy lifestyle, which the narrator identifies with leisure and philosophical contemplation. The narrator chooses this 'Life', and although it's a love of nature it isn't natural:

Death	Life
Nature	Life
Cold	Hot

We have included the warmth of the 'fire of Life' and the cold that comes when 'it sinks' – that is, the narrator dies. It's a small detail but that doesn't make it okay to leave it out.

You'll also have noticed that the 'nature' side of the opposition is explicitly privileged in the poem. The 'death' side seems also to be privileged. This is extremely surprising but it's quite in keeping with the regret-free acceptance of death that comes in the last line.

Work out a complete structure

A structuralist analysis is looking for <u>the</u> structure of the poem, not just 'some structures'. In 'Dying Speech of an Old Philosopher' the two apparently separate sets of oppositions are linked by this one: love/indifference. This is another important detail: the narrator 'loved' nature and art but considered the strivings of the human world unworthy of attention. Normally you'd oppose 'love' to 'hate', but there's nothing in the poem to suggest the narrator hates anything. The structure should be something you find in the poem, not something you impose on it from the outside.

Here's the structure:

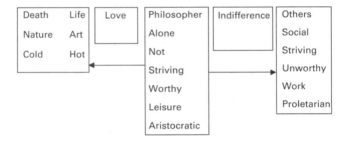

A diagram like this would be out of place in most essays; instead, you can use it as a map to guide you through the themes of the poem as you analyse it. This one indicates a stoical attitude, gladly embracing life and death equally and preferring contemplation to struggle. If you've been reading around (remember the advice right at the end of Chapter 1?) then you may know that this was related to the ancient philosophy of Stoicism, and you might mention that in your essay. Your essay will be well on its way to an 'A'.

No doubt you can see that this is a very complex poem indeed, and this structural analysis could give you a lot to say. So much for a nice simple example – but all structural analysis is like this. Because it forces you to be specific instead of vague, it helps you to see the subtleties, and subtleties are always more complicated than generalities.

Post-Structuralism?

The big claim that structuralism makes – to fully understand the basic structures at the heart of the things it studies – is flawed. This is because structuralism cannot account for everything in a poem. In the example above, it imposed 'the' structure on the poem, whereas there might be more than one way of looking at the poem. In addition, structuralism imposes neat oppositions where they might not actually be neat. Once this failure became clear, a new form of literary criticism grew up in a rather peculiar way.

Instead of dismissing structuralism and starting again from scratch, critics saw that it had its strengths, and that its flaws might be an extra asset. Post-structuralists typically do their structural analysis, but push it to the very limits so that it breaks down and reveals paradoxes or contradictions. Post-structuralists call these contradictions 'aporias' and some call what they do 'deconstruction'.

In 'Dying Speech of an Old Philosopher', you might be surprised to see 'love' linked with 'death' and 'cold' as well as 'hot' and 'life'. The narrator's attitude to death is actually more like indifference than love. This would be a good place to start looking very carefully at how these terms work in the poem.

These are two typical techniques employed in post-structuralist criticism:

- Looking at the way privilege works in the oppositions; is there some ambiguity? Does the poem try to privilege one but actually end up privileging the other? (For example, is it life or death that is really privileged in 'Dying Speech of an Old Philosopher'?
- 'Collapsing' the oppositions – do they really stay as neatly opposed as they seem to, or does the distinction between the two terms tend to get blurred?

This isn't the place to go into post-structuralism in detail: it's a complex field of work and the critical texts themselves are often forbiddingly difficult to understand. That shouldn't stop you from using structural analysis in a critical way. Paradoxes and contradictions in the structure can be points of interest rather than just problems to be solved. Post-structuralists sometimes approach texts this way:

1. The structural analysis reveals what the poem is trying to say (not what the poet is trying to say).
2. The failure of the structural analysis reveals the way language's complexities prevent the poem from saying exactly what it wants to.

Instead of this meaning the poem is a failure, though, it makes it all the more interesting. Remember, we're not making value judgements here.

Tutorial

Studying Structural Analysis

Questions

1. What does 'structuralism' mean? What about 'post-structuralism'?
2. Define 'binary opposition' and give five examples not used in this chapter.
3. What three steps might a simple structural analysis take?
4. What's an aporia? How might you find one?

Discussion Point

Are structures of binary oppositions really there in the poem? Or are they just a helpful aid to 'close reading'?

Practical Assignment

Look out for binary oppositions in all kinds of things – adverts, films, newspaper articles or any short text you come across. See if they fit into a structure that is more complex than just a single chain of associated terms.

> **Study Tip**
> Read some Lévi-Strauss. Don't worry about understanding it all – just get a feel for how really world-class structural analysis is done.

Writing an Essay on a Poem

One-minute overview

Essay writing is itself an art form and writing about poetry poses its own special challenges. Although examination and coursework conditions are very different, the basic ingredients of a good essay don't change. They are a single, clear idea and a structure that explains the idea and presents evidence that it's a sensible one.

A literary critic is like a barrister arguing a case in court. The issue must be clearly defined and as simple as possible; the argument must present evidence relevant to the case in a convincing way.

The particular problems associated with 'unseen' exams, 'compare and contrast' questions and writing about an individual poet need thought, as each requires a slightly different approach.

In this chapter you will learn:

- how to plan an essay
- what are the most common mistakes and how to avoid them
- how to add that extra 'something'.

Planning the Essay

The secret of a good essay is planning. Even in a timed exam, when every second is important, you should take five minutes to plan out each essay.

An essay should never feel aimless, and only the most desperate students write disjointed analyses that angle for point-scoring rather than making a coherent argument. Only the most desperate – and those who don't know any better.

Having an Idea

An essay must have at its centre a good, simple idea. Here are some examples from this book:

- 'The Phoenix and the Turtle' is a highly formalised, Classical poem.
- 'England in 1819' is torn between nostalgia and hope for the future.
- The relationship between man and God in 'When I Consider How My Light is Spent' is more complex than it first appears.
- The stoical outlook of 'Dying Speech of an Old Philosopher' collapses under the weight of its own rhetoric.

These ideas are given in order of sophistication. The first essay would simply describe the poem's features. The second finds a conflict within the poem, which is a more interesting approach. The third would explain the theme but then put a twist in the tail: all is not as it seems. This is much better. The fourth would do the same, but with its focus squarely on the language of the text; it might even find some self-referentiality in the poem (see Chapter 6), which would be better still.

Any of these ideas would be perfectly acceptable, but an idea with a twist or surprise is much better than a simple explanation. Remember that you're trying to reveal the complexities within a poem. A 'twist' doesn't disprove everything you've said before – that would be silly. It says: what we've seen up to now is okay, but really things are more complicated than that. In a standard essay you can't say anything extremely detailed and complex; what you can do is give an interesting account of the poem and reveal that this account doesn't exhaust the poem. There's more underneath the surface and you're a smart enough literary critic to know that. That's why a twist is so valuable to you, both in terms of honesty (you admit your interpretation isn't complete) and in terms of marks.

If your analysis only gives you an explanation, ask yourself whether there is anything in the detail of the poem that might add a new level of complexity, even if it calls your initial ideas into question. Look hard enough and you'll almost always find something that will overturn your simple explanation and make for a more complicated understanding of the text.

Saying it in a Sentence

These four ideas were all written in one (relatively short) sentence. This is important. Your essay needs a sort of slogan or catchphrase that will help keep you focused as you write it. If your 'single idea' is actually two or three ideas, it won't do that for you. Work out an overall concept that your essay is setting out to examine.

Organising the Evidence

Now you have your idea, select only the relevant evidence. It's tempting to include any information that you think is quite clever; if it doesn't relate to your central idea, throw it away or change the idea.

You should always go from simple to more complex. Start with your most straightforward information about the poem and proceed to more advanced stuff. If your idea includes a 'twist' be sure to clearly separate in your own mind which analytical points should go before the twist and which should come after the twist.

It's fine to revisit an analysis later in the essay. For example, you might give a general metrical analysis, explaining that the poem is very regular, but then later re-analyse one line to show that it's an exception. This might be the very thing that creates the 'twist'.

Planning your Paragraphs

Paragraphs in an essay are steps of your argument. Each one should take the reader a little further on. They should be quite long – much longer than the ones in this book. Go for around 200 words in each one if your essay is of an average length (1200–1500 words). If it's shorter, use shorter paragraphs. If it's longer you'd normally go for more paragraphs, not longer ones.

You can say quite a lot with each paragraph. Each one should be structured roughly like this:

1. One or two sentences introducing the idea for this paragraph.
2. Analytical evidence to support and develop the idea.
3. One or two sentences to sum it up.

Obviously you needn't stick rigidly to this, but do be sure to give your paragraphs a beginning, a middle and an end. Here's an example plan in note form:

1. Core sets of oppositions in 'Dying Speech of an Old Philosopher'– explain the basic theme.
2. Introduce the second theme – life/death and nature/art oppositions.
3. Problem – how do these two themes relate? Show they do relate (line two).
4. Introduce the third theme – love/indifference – which explains the relationship.
5. BUT the hot/cold opposition seems to undermine this picture.

Notice how the twist is clearly marked in the last paragraph.

Don't forget to introduce and conclude

Your whole essay will need an introduction and conclusion too. These will be the first and last paragraphs. The introduction should clearly state your idea, although you needn't give away all your surprises there. The conclusion should sum up everything you've already said. Don't put any analytical evidence in either of these paragraphs; use them for more general material. Remember the first rule of public speaking:

- Tell the audience what you're going to say (introduction).
- Tell them the facts (main part of the essay).
- Tell them what you've told them (conclusion).

People – even intelligent people – can be pretty stupid sometimes, and this kind of approach will help them understand exactly what you've tried to do. If your essay confuses them they might easily assume it's because you're confused.

You'll usually find these paragraphs are a bit shorter. Do avoid making them too cursory, though, because your reader needs the introduction to get an idea of what is going to happen, and the conclusion to tie everything up.

Writing the Essay

Just like writing for a newspaper or an advertisement, you need to tailor your style to the situation. Since the situation is academic scholarship, keep it formal. The best way to learn the style is to read up-to-date literary criticism. There are many turns of phrase which you'll pick up that way and which will make your writing more professional.

Who should you aim your writing at? How much do you need to explain? Make your 'imaginary reader' an intelligent fellow student. Don't assume that your tutors know everything – they don't – but don't insult their intelligence either.

Making your Case

In the introduction say clearly what your central idea is. You can take more than a sentence over it, but if you have a 'twist' in your argument it's better not to blurt it out here. That would be rather like someone telling you the ending of a film when it's only just started. You can say something like, 'The structure of the poem, however, considerably complexifies this situation'. This will hopefully intrigue your reader without giving the game away.

In each paragraph you should present evidence that you hope will convince the reader about your interpretation. Imagine that the reader is a bit sceptical and you need to try hard to make your case compelling. Try to think of objections that your reader might make so you can pre-empt them in your essay. The more you practise anticipating these kinds of criticisms, the tighter your writing will get.

Using Quotations

The more often you quote the poem in support of your argument, the more convincing it will be. The best essays seem to let the text speak for itself. Use quotation often and extensively.

Don't put words into the poet's mouth. In 'Dying Speech of an Old Philosopher' the poem says 'strife', use that word, in quotation marks, wherever possible. Don't use 'work' or 'effort' unless you have a specific point to make, because they have slightly different meanings and those variations can be very important. Some students end up analysing a poem they've re-written without meaning to because they haven't used enough quotations.

In an essay on a short poem you can account for every word in it, but if your subject is longer you might not be able to. In that case, selective quotation is very important. Avoid quoting ten lines when two will do – the result could easily confuse your reader. You can assume that your reader has a copy of the poem to hand while reading your essay, so a line reference will suffice. If the poem is an obscure one of your own choosing you could include a photocopy for your reader so your quotations can be precise and to the point.

Comparing Two Poems

It's very common in exams to be asked to 'compare', 'contrast' or 'compare and contrast' two poems. Often these will be by the same poet or on the same subject.

Whichever of the three questions is asked, you should both compare (finding things in common) and contrast (finding differences). Here's how to weight your answer:

Question says	Your essay should have
'Compare'	a longer first section of comparisons, but a final paragraph or two of contrasts.
'Contrast'	a longer first section of contrasts, but a final paragraph or two of comparisons.
'Compare and contrast'	EITHER first half comparisons and second half contrasts OR each paragraph finds something that seems to be shared but is actually contrasting (or vice versa).

Make sure you give equal space to both poems and remember to have an idea and make a plan – don't just write random comparisons or contrasts. Notice how in each of these approaches your essay gets a nice 'twist' even though the question itself just asks you to do something straightforward. This is the kind of thing that will earn you marks, especially in an exam.

Writing about a Poet

If you're studying a particular poet, you obviously can't write an analysis of every poem they wrote. At the same time you shouldn't just write on one poem and, of course, you must avoid analysing the poet instead of the poems.

The best way to approach this problem is to write about common themes or techniques (or both and how they're related, which is better) in the poet's work by using three or four examples. Make sure there's some variety among the poems you choose unless you're writing about a specific area of the poet's work (such as Shakespeare's sonnets).

Example: Swinburne

Your central idea might be something like 'Swinburne's poetry is often consumed by a dark vision of nature'. Then you would carefully pick three or four poems. Perhaps you'd choose these:

- 'By the North Sea' – description of wild, dangerous nature, compared with God BUT result is sinister and definitely not Romantic.
- 'The Sundew' – about a carnivorous plant – subject is romantic love BUT the relationship with nature is paradoxical and undercuts this theme.
- 'Euridice' – a re-telling of a Classical myth, BUT the poem becomes obsessed with a violent image of childbirth.
- It is a good idea to give each poem two paragraphs – one for straight explanation and one for the 'twist'. This progress – from obvious nature poem to a poem that has similar themes but at a less obvious level – works nicely. You don't need to claim that the theme appears in all his poetry, just that it's there in some poems and not just in the obvious ones.

Tips for Essay Writing in Exams

Those who succeed under exam conditions are those who stick to a few simple, common-sense rules. Here they are.

Time Management

- Divide your time equally. If you have three hours to write four essays, spend 45 minutes on each essay. Five minutes for planning leaves you 40 minutes of writing time – so after 25 minutes you should be halfway through your essay.
- Watch the clock and be disciplined. If you're running out of time, wind up the essay and get started on the next one.
- Write the required number of essays. It's astonishing how many students sit down to a four-question exam and turn in two excellent essays. It's virtually impossible to pass an exam that way. Even if you got 70% for each essay (that's an extremely high mark) your mark for the exam would be 35% – a fail.
- You can't afford a ten-minute cigarette break. If you smoke, use patches or gum (if it's allowed) during the exam or, better still, give up smoking.

What to Write

- Read the question. If you don't like the way it's worded, use your introduction to twist it around to accommodate what you want to say. But DON'T ignore it or misread it.

- Examiners are looking for structured, intelligent, well-written work, not scrappy notes or random musings. Work to the same standard as you do for coursework. Five minutes' planning at the start is time very well spent – use it to structure your paragraphs in an intelligent way.

- Examiners want to see evidence of your own original thought. They want to see something different, unusual and even surprising.

- Assuming you've followed all of the above, the longer your essay is, the more marks you're likely to get. Examiners are looking for reasons to give you marks, but you have to say something to get a mark for it. DON'T let this lead you into a scatter-gun, throw-enough-and-hope-some-sticks approach, but DO write fast and furiously.

Exam Conditions

Exams are hard physical work. Eat properly before going in and don't have a hangover. It is advisable at least three weeks before an examination period to 'detox'. Cut down on drinking and make sure you eat healthily. On the morning of the examination it is extremely important to have a sensible breakfast. Think of yourself as an athlete about to perform; you owe it to yourself to prepare thoroughly and that includes making sure you eat the right food, because food is your fuel for peak performance.

If you feel ill be sure to mention it to someone before the exam starts. If you can, get a doctor's note either beforehand or immediately afterwards.

You should be hyped enough to keep going without a break but if you do find yourself flagging, spend two or three minutes just staring into space. It relaxes your eyes and refreshes your concentration. If you get writer's cramp, spread out your hand flat on the table, palm down and fingers apart. Rest it there for 10–20 seconds and the ache should subside.

There's such a thing as being too laid back in an exam. A little adrenaline will help you. If you suffer from more serious nerves, though, the best thing you can do for yourself is prepare by practising writing the kinds of essays you will be expected to produce in the exam. Give yourself a time limit. The first few you try might be a nasty shock, but it's better to get that nasty shock now than on results day. If you can honestly tell yourself that you're well prepared for an exam, the nerves should all but evaporate.

Tutorial

Studying Essay Writing

Questions

1. What should an ideal paragraph contain (assuming it's not the introduction or the conclusion)?

2. List some sensible exam techniques, under these three headings:

   a) Time management.

   b) What to write.

   c) Exam conditions.

They don't have to be the same as what's in this chapter.

Discussion Point

Is one exam technique suitable for everyone, or do individuals work better in different ways? Discuss your own approaches to exams – both good and bad – and you'll probably discover some useful ideas.

Practical Assignments

1. Reading other students' essays is an excellent way to put yourself in your tutors' shoes. You could even exchange essays with peers on a regular basis. Most exams aren't marked competitively, and so exchanging ideas can only benefit everybody.

2. If you're having trouble getting motivated for an exam, do a timed essay on a short poem plucked at random from an anthology. You may get a fright.

Study Tips

- Plan essays even if you don't write them. They're useful revision aids and the practice is good in itself.
- If you have to sit formal exams, get hold of as many past papers as possible. Do it now, regardless of how long remains before you have to sit the exams. You may find that similar questions crop up year in, year out; use them in your preparation but be prepared for something different too. Students can get caught out predicting questions: especially when the same topic comes up on every paper for years. We know of one student who practised this approach and only revised for one question. In the examination, when he turned over the question paper, it wasn't there. That mistake probably cost him a whole grade in the exam.

10 **Making Presentations**

One-minute overview

Many courses now expect students to make a presentation as part of the learning opportunities given in the course. It is also true that making presentations of your own ideas is becoming extremely important in both industry and academia, with many organisations making it a standard procedure for the introduction of new ideas or procedures in working practice. So in many ways this is now becoming an essential skill. There are numerous occasions where people have to sit through boring presentations that are frankly a waste of time because the presenter fails to deliver his or her message in a meaningful way, or the audience leaves without taking on board the message and without any intention to act on the message.

In this chapter you will learn:
- why making presentations is a positive learning experience
- how to plan and prepare for a top presentation
- techniques to help your presentation go well
- how to overcome nerves and other problems.

Focus Points

Giving a presentation is a positive learning experience. It's an opportunity for you to 'shine' in front of your peers. One of the best pieces of advice for anyone giving a presentation is to ensure that you enjoy the experience. It's also a major learning experience for you so it really is worth the effort to do it well.

Giving presentations develops personal transferable skills that include:

- making a verbal case
- presenting yourself as a credible authoritative figure to others
- persuading others by the quality of your arguments
- developing the self-confidence to stand up in front of a group of people and address them with authority
- positively using non-verbal behaviour as part of your presentation
- anticipating and dealing with negative responses
- answering questions.

Planning and Preparing

There is no doubt that there is a link between well-prepared presentations and effective presentations. A well-prepared presentation does not guarantee success, but it does increase the probability that you will be successful.

When you are planning a presentation make sure that you:

- understand the nature of your audience
- identify the aims and objectives of your presentation
- research the topic and create a structure for your presentation
- rehearse your presentation

The Nature of Your Audience

It's no good planning a degree-level presentation for a group of 14-year olds who have never studied the subject at that level. So it is vital that you have an understanding of the people to whom you will be talking. In a sixth form the audience is likely to be other students; in a college or university the same is true but it may also include top-level academics. It is always a good tip, if you are addressing a group with a well-known academic present, to include a quote from him/her.

You must create your presentation for your audience and therefore you must determine their characteristics and their possible needs. Ask yourself some key questions.

- What is their age range?
- What is their general education level?
- How much do they already know?
- How much do you expect them to take away?
- Are they willing participants or have they been forced to
- attend?

Aims and Objectives

You need to be clear in your own mind what you are trying to achieve. What is the aim of the presentation?

- Define your desired outcome in terms of your audience; what do you want them to take away from your presentation?
- How can this desired outcome be best achieved?
- What are the main points that you need to make?
- How can you check that your aims and objectives have been reached?

Topic Research

No matter how familiar you believe you are with the material in your proposed presentation, it really is advisable to check your research and ensure it comes from more than one source. Examine the evidence you gather in your research and make sure that it is valid/reliable and objective. It is worth visualising the presentation as a member of the audience. Ask yourself what they will see, hear and remember.

Providing Structure

Structure is important because it enables you to impart information in a logical manner and it helps the audience to understand what you are saying. Split your presentation into three main sections:

- The introduction
- The development
- The summary.

It is essential that you know exactly what length of time you have to deliver the presentation and that you stick to it.

Make sure the material is:

- concise, clear and relevant.
- logically sequenced.
- condensed in interim summaries.

> **Note**
>
> Including humour in a presentation is difficult; what you find funny isn't necessarily what others find funny. If you must include humour then there are some guidelines that you need to consider. Use cartoons or photographs that may make your audience laugh, but avoid telling jokes unless you are a talented comic. You should also avoid jokes at your own expense; one of your key objectives should be to present yourself as a person of expertise. You do not further this objective by setting yourself up as a joke.

Rehearsing

Visualisation means rehearsing your talk in your head. There is clear evidence that people who visualise their presentations actually deliver a far better presentation at the end. Visualisation is a common practice with athletes; they are encouraged to think of how they will feel when they win. They literally experience the euphoria of winning and imagine all of the experiences that go with winning. This is what you need to do with your presentation.

Techniques

Audio Visual Aids

Consider using Powerpoint™ – but not in the way that is commonly used. There are far too many slide shows where the presenter literally reads the slides to the audience, and they are the most boring presentations you can imagine. One of the best slide shows we ever witnessed was by a presenter in the Westcountry of England. Instead of the usual dry sentences he used photographs and speech bubbles. The audience was spellbound by what each photo meant and how it added to their knowledge of the subject. In this way he built in his humour without diminishing his own standing as an authority on the subject. It also meant that the photos he chose acted as prompts for his talk.

Remembering

The best-prepared presentation can fall apart if you forget key facts or the order in which they should be imparted. Try using cue cards or mnemonics to aid your memory. Another useful technique to recall information is the Roman room method. Simply imagine a journey you know well. With each significant place on the journey, associate a piece of important material. When you recall the journey you should be able to recall the information.

Aspects of Speech

It may sound obvious, but you need to ensure that your speech is clear. Regional accents are no longer an issue as long as you pronounce words correctly and in a manner that the audience can understand. Use varying tones throughout your talk and emphasise important points. There is nothing more boring than listening to a monotone voice. You should also avoid reading the slides to your audience. This happens when the presenter hasn't thought through what they want to say. Most adults can read; they want you to talk to them and treat them like intelligent adults. Do use bullet points on slides to prompt what you have to say, but make sure YOU interact with the slide. Use images or characters and speech bubbles to make a statement that you can interact with; this makes your presentation far more memorable and satisfies the objectives set at the start.

NVC (non-verbal communication)

Mannerisms like smoothing your hair or scratching your chin can distract from the message you are trying to give. Make sure you give a genuine smile and look people directly in the eye.

Overcoming Problems

Nerves

Standing in front of a group of people can be intimidating. Use simple techniques to make you feel better. For instance, if you feel intimated by the audience then imagine them sitting on a toilet with their underwear around their ankles. There is no way they can be threatening now (just don't giggle in front of them – it will give you away).

Dealing with Questions

It is sometimes difficult to predict the questions you will be asked. Make and memorise a list of the key points regarding your presentation, and include a brief biography of the poet or poets for your own background knowledge. For instance, if your talk is on Hardy, make sure that you have his birth and death dates, the names of both of his wives and the titles of his key books and poems. This could be on a small mind map on an index card. If someone asks you for some biographical information, you have the facts at hand. Having said that, never be afraid to admit that you do not know. The way to deal with this is to say, 'leave me your details and I will find out for you'. This reassures the audience member that you are professional and will satisfy their requirements.

Heckling

Heckling can happen and it is unpleasant, so you need to deal with it firmly but courteously. You can use strategies like I'm glad you made that point, I did intend to mention it later'. You can then put it to the audience that 'if you wish me to deal with this matter now, I will, but I was intending to cover...' Then firmly say, 'may I suggest that we cover that later?', smile and move on.

Further Reading

This chapter has covered the main points of giving a presentation, but for more detail read *Study Skills: Maximise Your Time to Pass Exams* by John Kennedy, published by Studymates.

Useful Websites

On the day we visited these sites working well and were worthy of recommendation. This is only a sample of what is available but hopefully it will help you to start using the internet as a learning resource. However, neither Studymates Limited, the author nor any/all of their agents can be held responsible for the consequences of actions taken by the reader. Readers are advised to take appropriate professional advice before entering into any arrangements.

African American Women Writers of the 19th Century

http://digital.nypl.org/schomburg/writers aa19/
If you are studying American literature then this site is a must.

They say:
'The 19th century was a formative period in African-American literary and cultural history. Prior to the Civil War, the majority of black Americans living in the United States were held in bondage. Law and practice forbade teaching blacks from learning to read or write. Even after the war, many of the impediments to learning and literary productivity remained. Nevertheless, black men and women of the 19th century learned to both read and write. Moreover, more African-Americans than we yet realise turned their observations, feelings, social viewpoints and creative impulses into published works. In time, this 19th-century printed record included poetry, short stories, histories, narratives, novels, autobiographies, social criticism and theology, as well as economic and philosophical treatises. Unfortunately, much of this body of literature remained, until very recently, relatively inaccessible to 20th-century scholars, teachers, creative artists and others interested in black life. Prior to the late 1960s, most Americans (black as well as white) had never heard of these 19th-century authors, much less read their works.'

Are there Ciphers in Shakespeare?

http://home.att.net/~tleary/
This site really makes you think.

They say:
'This is an introduction to an ingenious and creative cipher system to be found in the works of William Shakespeare. This work questions whether or not Shakespeare wrote the works attributed to him. It particularly examines the works for possible ciphers (codes) used to hint at Francis Bacon as the actual author.'

Anthology of Middle English Literature

http://www.luminarium.org/medlit
Covers a list of 'names' including Chaucer, but it does have rather irritating music that has to be turned off.

The quotes section is particularly useful and should save you time.

British Comparative Literature Association

http://www.bc1a.org/index.htm

They say:
'The British Comparative Literature Association (BCLA), founded in 1975, aims to promote the scholarly study of literature without confinement to national and linguistic boundaries, and in relation to other disciplines. The BCLA's primary interests are in literature, the contexts of literature and the interaction between literatures.'

British Women Romantic Poets, 1789–1832

http://digital.lib.ucdavis.edu/projects/bwrp/index.htm
This is a US site that is worked on by scholars in the US and Canada. It is an excellent contribution to women's studies.

Comparative Literature

http://darkwing.uoregon.edu/~clj/
This is the website for the official journal of the American
Comparative Literature Association

Comparative Literature Studies

http://www.cl-studies.org/

They say:
*'Comparative Literature Studies is a journal devoted to the
comparative research in literary history, the history of ideas,
critical theory, studies between authors and literary relations
within and beyond the Western tradition.'*

Critical Reading: a Guide

http://www.brocku.ca/english/jlye/criticalreading.html
This site was created by Professor John Lye and is an absolute
must for poetry students. Make sure you bookmark this site.

They say:
*'This is a guide to what you might look for in analysing literature,
particularly poetry and fiction. An analysis explains what a work
of literature means, and how it means it; it is essentially an
articulation of and a defence of an interpretation which shows how
the resources of literature are used to create the meaningfulness of
the text. There are people who resist analysis, believing that it 'tears
apart' a work of art; however a work of art is an artifice, that is, it
is made by someone with an end in view: as a made thing, it can
be and should be analysed as well as appreciated.'*

Critical Theory

http://www.uta.edu/huma/illuminations

They say:
*'The Critical Theory Website is a research resource for those
interested in the Critical Theory project. Firmly based in*

Frankfurt School thought, this site maintains a collection of articles, excerpts and chapters from many contemporary writers of and about critical theory. Additional submissions from graduate students and others are also available, as are links to other websites and related sources.'

CyberEnglish

http://www.tnellen.com/cybereng/
Some goodies for English teachers here and it is a must for student teachers.

Exploring Literature

http://www.shared-visions.com/explore/literature/lithome .htm
You must visit this site if only to read the articles, especially 'How To Get Better Marks With Less Work.'

International Comparative Literature Association

http://icla.byu.edu/www/
This website looks very corporate but that is not always a bad thing.

They say:
'Welcome to the International Comparative Literature Association page. This page is designed to be a source for information about the ICLA and its organisation and membership. Since its establishment in 1954, the Association has been a major proponent of international research in the field of comparative literature.'

Texts and Documents: Europe

http://history.hanover.edu/project.html#modern

They say:
'This page provides excellent links for all the major literary periods as well as the e-texts for many works. Look at this page for relevant historical, cultural, religious and political background information on medieval, Renaissance, 18th century, Victorian and modern literature.'

Literary Periods
http://www.bedfordstmartins.com/litLinks/periods/modern.htm

Poetry Analysis Fact Sheet
http://www.tnellen.com/cybereng/analysis html

Techniques for Poetry Analysis
http://www.pfmb.uni-mb.si/eng/dept/eng/poetry/text/techniqu.htm

Poetry Analysis: a Step-By-Step Approach
http://www.lakelandschools.org/EDTECH/Inspiration/poetry.htm/
This is worth seeing just to look at the diagrammatic break down of all the steps in analysing a poem. It is superb.

Poetry Analysis
http://www.ccel.org/h/herbert/temple/poetry.html
A very dense site but with some goodies, so it is worth the effort.

Poetry Magic
www.poetrymagic.co.uk/critiquing.html
This website has an excellent checklist for poetry criticism.

Poems and Quotes
http://www.poems-and-quotes.com/

Playwrights on the Web
http://www.stageplays.com/writers.htm

Post Modern Culture
http://www3.iath.virginia.edu/pmc/readings.html

Postmodernism and its Critics
http://www.as.ua.edu/ant/Faculty/murphy/436/pomo.htm
This site veers off into anthropological studies BUT it is by students for students, and there is some good information here.

Society for Critical Exchange
http://www.case.edu/affil/sce/

They say:
'*The SCE is North America's oldest scholarly organisation devoted to theory. Our various interdisciplinary projects, conferences and symposia serve to advance the role of theory in academic and intellectual arenas. Our projects encompass a broad spectrum of disciplines, most prominently literary studies, legal studies and practices, economics, composition and pedagogy.*

This website includes current information about our programs and projects. It will soon include the extensive archives of past SCE projects, as well as the history of the SCE.'

Sylvia Plath Forum
http://www.sylviaplathforum.com/analysis.html

The Bluestocking Archive
http://www.faculty.umb.edu/elizabeth_fay//archive2.html

They say:
'*This archive assumes a deep relation between the intellectual and social movement of the Bluestockings, the culture and cult of Sensibility and High Romanticism. It is an archive of texts by or relating to the 18th-century British Bluestocking Circle and the second generation Blues, including predecessor texts, and literature of sensibility as it is derived from the Bluestockings' concerns with aesthetics, and with women's aesthetic achievements.*'

Tracy Duckart's Instructional Website at Humboldt State University
http://www.humboldt.edu/~tdd2/PoetryAnalysis.htm
This is worthy of your time. Well done to Tracy Duckart and thank you.

The Poetry Society
http://www.poetrysociety.org.uk/
This is a delightful website and if you are serious about poetry, you should consider joining.

They say:

'The Poetry Society is a membership-based and Arts Council England-funded registered charity, whose stated aims are to promote the study, use and enjoyment of poetry. It was founded in 1909 and is due to celebrate its centenary in 2009.

Many professional poets are members of the Society, although not all. Out membership is open to anyone. Many of our thousands of members around the world are teachers, librarians, booksellers, journalists – a wide range, in fact, of readers, writers and lovers of poetry.'

The Victorian Literary Studies Archive
http://www.lang.nagoya-u.ac.jp/~matsuoka/Victorian.html

The Web Concordances

www.dundee.ac.uk/english/wics/wics/htm
You can download your own software to create your own Concordance and there are workbooks for you to use. This is an excellent resource for students.

They say:
'A concordance is a comprehensive index of the words used in a text or a body of texts. Usually there are also citations of the passages in which the words occur. Its simplest use is as an index, to locate quickly any passage in a text. All you need to know is one word from the passage: look up that word in a concordance to the text and you will find the passage.

But a concordance does much more than this. What you find when you look up any word is a gathering-together o/all the usages of that word. Straight away you can compare all the contexts in which the word is used. This often enables special insights into the particular meanings of a text and into its characteristic language. For literary, legal or philosophical texts, where language and meaning are primary concerns, the concordance is one of the most powerful investigative tools available.'

Index